Mapping Motivation for Coaching

Mapping Motivation for Coaching, co-written with Bevis Moynan, is the first of a series of six books that are all linked to the author's Motivational Map toolkit. Each book builds on a different aspect of personal, team, and organisational development. This book is a practical guide to understanding how personal and career development is underpinned by motivation, and how coaching and mapping are perfectly complementary activities. More specifically, it shows how using Motivational Maps within an accepted coaching framework can not only accelerate the process in order to achieve results for the client more quickly, but also go deeper, both in mutual understanding and also the possibility of facilitating a successful outcome; for the client not only needs to understand their issue more effectively through the coaching process, but also needs to be motivated to want to take significant action to deal with it.

Understanding, then, is one thing, but having the energy for follow-through is another, and it is precisely in this area that combining Maps with coaching techniques is so powerful. This highly original approach will enable all coaches everywhere in the world to get into the heart of their clients' issues faster, better, and be able to help them solve these issues more easily.

James Sale is the Creative Director of Motivational Maps Ltd, a training company that he co-founded in 2006.

Bevis Moynan is the Director of Magenta Coaching Solutions, a company focusing on coaching and training excellent coaches, therapists, trainers, and consultants.

The Complete Guide to Mapping Motivation

Motivation is the fuel that powers all our endeavours, whether they be individual, team, or organisational. Without motivation we are bound to achieve far less than we really could, and without motivation we will fall short of what we are truly capable of. Motivation, before the creation by James Sale of Motivational Maps, has always been a 'flaky', subjective, and impressionistic topic, and so-called 'motivational speakers' are perhaps rightly not considered entirely credible. But the Motivational Map has provided both language and metrics by which motivation can now be fully understood, described, and utilised effectively. The Complete Guide to Mapping Motivation provides a total overview of how motivation informs all the critical activities that we and teams and organisations undertake at work. This includes how motivation is vital to the individual on a personal level if they want to be happy and fulfilled; it includes its applications in the domains of coaching, engagement, leadership, performance appraisal, team building, and organisational development and change. So much has been written in the last 30 years about behaviours that often the literature has missed the crucial point: What drives the behaviours? This new model, then, instead of trying to control behaviours, seeks to understand motivators so that everyone can reach their full potential, not via command and control, but through bottom-up collaboration and appropriate reward strategies.

The Complete Guide to Mapping Motivation is a ground-breaking, innovative, and new approach to managing motivation in the workplace. As such it is an essential series of books for all leaders, managers, and key personnel engaged in improving how individuals, teams and whole organisations can be more effective, productive, and engaged – and how they can want all of these things too.

For a complete list of titles in this series, please visit https://www.routledge.com/ The-Complete-Guide-to-Mapping-Motivation/book-series/MAPMOTIVAT

Mapping Motivation for Coaching
James Sale and Bevis Moynan

Mapping Motivation for Coaching

James Sale and Bevis Moynan

For June :   ! ! !
Thank you ! ! !

Sale
19/9/19

Lovely to see you again ☺

Routledge
Taylor & Francis Group
LONDON AND NEW YORK

First published 2018
by Routledge
2 Park Square, Milton Park, Abingdon, Oxon OX14 4RN

and by Routledge
711 Third Avenue, New York, NY 10017

Routledge is an imprint of the Taylor & Francis Group, an informa business

British Library Cataloguing-in-Publication Data
A catalogue record for this book is available from the British Library

Library of Congress Cataloging-in-Publication Data
Names: Sale, James, author. | Moynan, Bevis, author.
Title: Mapping motivation for coaching/James Sale and Bevis Moynan.
Description: Abingdon, Oxon ; New York, NY : Routledge, 2018. |
Includes index.
Identifiers: LCCN 2017044397 | ISBN 9780815367536 (hardback)
Subjects: LCSH: Personal coaching.
Classification: LCC BF637.P36 S25 2018 | DDC 158.3—dc23
LC record available at https://lccn.loc.gov/2017044397

ISBN: 978-0-8153-6753-6 (hbk)
ISBN: 978-1-351-25712-1 (ebk)

Typeset in Times New Roman
by Apex CoVantage, LLC

MIX
Paper from
responsible sources
FSC
www.fsc.org   FSC™ C013985

Printed in the United Kingdom
by Henry Ling Limited

Dedicated to Piyawat James Sale and Jules Moynan

Contents

Figures

Preface

Mapping Motivation for Coaching is a practical guide to understanding how personal and career development is underpinned by motivation, and how coaching and Motivational Mapping ("Mapping") are perfectly complementary activities. Also, this work is cumulative: it builds on the foundation of *Mapping Motivation*,[1] the primary source book published by Gower in 2016. But it is also a standalone, and one need not have read the previous book in order to derive enormous benefit from this one. Those readers, however, who have the Expert motivator in their top three profile will almost certainly want to study the former publication after they complete this volume, if only to deepen their understanding further!

But having referred to the "Expert" motivator in their top three profile, we are immediately guilty of using the jargon – the lingo – of Motivational Maps before having explained it in an ordered sequence. So, each book in the new *Complete Guide to Mapping Motivation* series will contain a brief introductory and summary chapter explaining the basics of Motivational Maps; this will be distilled from *Mapping Motivation*. This overview of the Motivational Maps' structure and meaning should enable any coach to be able to understand pretty quickly what this is all about.

It is also important to say at this point – given the limitations of space in this (or any) book – that we are not attempting to cover how to be a coach in its entirety. There are other books on the market that do that, and we refer to some of them in our text, and there is more follow-through information at the end. No, the key to understanding what this book is fundamentally about is this: if you currently are a coach, or if you are a manager who actively coaches others within your organisation, or even if you are a manager with wide experience of using coaches and maybe seeking to change career and become a coach yourself, then this book is for you; it is also for the reader who may not be a professional coach but wishes to self-coach and embark on some career or personal development. For all of you this book is a goldmine of information and techniques, any one of which might prove transformational. And underpinning it all is the Motivational Map, which we give full access to in note 12 of the Introduction – you may wish to go there immediately in order to activate your personal Motivational Map as a prelude to reading this book. Certainly, the contents will make even more sense to you if you do.

This leads on to one final point in this Preface: namely, that this book has not been written in a sequential way, but rather topologically; it is entirely possible to dip in and out of it as one's interests dictate. There are powerful ideas to be found here, as well as transformative techniques and tools to be deployed; some can be used in a standalone kind of way, others require Motivational Map technology. But we are not prescriptive; on the contrary, pragmatism rules – will it work for you? If so, use it. At the end of the day we all need to understand that management and psychological models are not reality[2]: they are a map of reality, and all maps suffer from the deficiency of being incomplete to a greater or lesser extent. As it happens, Motivational Maps, as a model, is extremely accurate,[3] and the results it produces at the individual level have been nothing short of astonishing and revelatory to the individuals concerned. We hope that you, too, will enjoy a similar sense of astonishment and revelation as you read through this work – and ultimately will want to become more involved.

Acknowledgements

All case studies and personal Maps cited in this book are based on real people and actual events; however, to preserve privacy and confidentiality, all have been anonymised. We would like to thank all those clients who have taught us so much about themselves, their businesses and how far Maps can help boost them and their performances.

In similar vein we would also like to thank all the licensees of Motivational Maps – over 400 worldwide – and especially our Senior Practitioners: Susannah and Heath, Kate, Jane, Mark, and Akeela who keep the flame full and burning.

Behind the scenes James Watson and Rob Breeds have provided invaluable support and advice and we are very grateful.

Linda E. Sale, the artist and Managing Director of Motivational Maps Ltd, has to be thanked for support and faith in the creation of this work so far reaching it cannot really be described; but what can be described is the fact that all the Figures in this book, and the cover illustration too, are her work. We are truly grateful – and in awe of her abilities.

Joy Bemrose for contributing to our research; all errors, are of course ours.

Notes

1 *Mapping Motivation*, James Sale, Gower (2016).
2 "A map is not the territory it represents, but, if correct, it has a similar structure to the territory, which accounts for its usefulness." - Alfred Korzybski, *Science and Sanity* (1933). This expression subsequently became a major principle underpinning Neuro Linguistic Programming (NLP), whose application we consider in much more detail in Chapter 4 of this book.
3 For example, Face Validity testing - which asks users of the Motivational Map to rate its accuracy - records a 95 per cent accuracy rating.

Introduction

Over the last 25 years or so coaching has become an activity that once was purely associated with sports, but which now has become a mainstay process for developing people in business and in their personal lives. Indeed, coaching and coaches have become ubiquitous; and to use the jargon of our times: coaching is a major growth industry. But reflecting back on its origins in sports is useful. Why do football teams, golfers, athletes, and every other type of physical competitor want – nay, need – a coach and often a series of specialist coaches? Because, put simply, it is quite clear that coaches can make a massive difference to the performance of their clients, and in making such a difference they can turn competitors into winners. When we enter the world of business, of organisations, of life itself, we find that there is increasing pressure for businesses and organisations to perform: to perform as an organisation, for each of its teams to perform, and at the granular level for each individual to perform. When they do, productivity increases, and when that increases, and the strategy for the business (and for non-profit organisations too) is right, then profits increase (or in the case of non-profit organisations, value is enhanced). We all want to enjoy success. Hence the increasingly central role of coaching. One interesting research statistic on this found that training alone increased productivity in organisations by 22.4 per cent, but that when coaching augmented the process the productivity increased to 88 per cent, nearly four times "the level achieved by training alone".[1] No wonder, then, that it has become so critical to organisational success.

So, coaching helps individuals (and so teams and organisations) perform at a higher level. For this reason, vast sums of money are spent on coaches and coaching programmes by organisations throughout the world.[2]

Two questions, however, emerge from this. The first is: but what is coaching? And the second is: what is performance, properly understood?

If we understood more clearly what constituted performance, then maybe that would help us when we discuss how coaching can drive and increase it. But there is more, and it is worth mentioning this now, as it is so critical to what an appreciation of coaching is. We will analyse performance more thoroughly in this book, but it is important to realise that every one of us starts off performing poorly!

We learn to ride a bike, and we fall off; we try to swim, and we sink; we want to spell a word or write a coherent sentence and when we start we appear dyslexic and confused. Gradually, through teaching and instruction, we 'get' some of these things and some of us can become excellent cyclists, swimmers, spellers, writers and ... anything else: strategists, marketers, leaders, sales people, computer programmers and so on.[3] But the point is, performance, which will define anon, is always, always, always preceded by development. Another word for this would be learning.

Interestingly, how many people do you often meet with a truly healthy appetite for failure? Not many, yet some of the most successful people on the planet openly exclaim they are where they are as a result of failing more frequently than anyone else![4] The key therefore is to take the learnings and move forward from failure; and, in fact, not to perceive it as failure but instead as a necessary, indeed essential process: we have to fail in order to learn, at least initially and maybe for quite some time. Many, however, through conditioning, hold onto negative emotion associated with poor performance, which leads to the only thing stopping the achievement of goals, namely, giving up!

Young children don't give up on walking; and if you are persistent with your own goals you will achieve them (maybe not in the timescale you prescribed, but you will get there), just as children learn all of the incredible complexity of information that they do in the first few years of life. Goal achievement is just as inevitable; in fact, humans are designed to achieve their goals as long as:

A)   they have a goal ...
B)   they constructively think or reflect upon it often ...
C)   they are persistent ....

This sounds simple; however, think about it for a minute. First, you might like to reflect on whether you have goals, whether you consistently think about them and whether or not you have been persistent in the pursuit of them? Also, what is it that causes us not to achieve our aspirations (ultimately us giving up, however we may try to blame others)? What is it that causes us to give up? Negative emotion! What is the source of negative emotion – negative thought! And whose thoughts are they? Mm, yes, our own. Indeed, thinking 'constructively' about our own goals is precisely what we often do not do.

Herein lies the hope for one of the more recent developments in coaching: the ability to provide clients with sufficient knowledge of their own thought processes so that they take 100 per cent responsibility for the outcome and accept the challenges, blocks, barriers and 'adversities' that arise.

It is important to stress at the outset that we can coach for performance, and we can also coach for development too. In one sense coaching for performance is easier. Why? Because it has an end point: if you are coached on how to improve your golf stroke or how to improve your butterfly motion in the water, then once it is done, it is done. But to coach for development can be more open-ended and actually more profound, for we are helping the individual learn how to learn and go on learning indefinitely, to become more self-sufficient and so live a more fulfilled life – one more capable of being independent and unintimidated by the circumstances around that beset all of us from time to time.

To return, then, to the central question: what is coaching? There are many models of coaching: for example, traditionally the GROW[5] model has been very popular and over recent times other models have found their place and begun to have an impact. Also, Neuro Linguistic Programming (NLP) works to remove subconscious blockages to performance. Its principles operate at a more developmental level, aiming to assist each individual to be more consciously aware of their own thought processes. Alongside these, we should not underestimate the impact of some of the more holistic therapeutic practices that may not, initially, seem overtly to be linked to coaching. All good coaches at some point experience a client who has a block impeding performance, and those coaches who either broaden their training or experience, or who work in conjunction with other specialists, can and do have the largest positive impact with their clients.

Professor Nigel MacLennan, however, defines it this way:

> Coaching is the process whereby one individual helps another: to unlock their natural ability; to perform, learn and achieve; to increase awareness of the factors which determine performance; to increase their sense of self-responsibility and ownership of their performance; to self-coach; to identify and remove internal barriers to achievement.[6]

Wow – this is very all-encompassing and powerful. But notice some central issues here: coaching is one-on-one, somebody is being helped (so it's not training); it's about raising one's game by unlocking potential through learning and so performing in order to achieve more (so it's teleological and has the end in mind) and it has a strong personal flavour (one needs to take responsibility at all times for one's learning and one's results). In a way it's like 'growing up' all over again. We take it for granted that children have to grow up and they do that by learning; we can so easily become adults and think we know all we need to know.

Many people switch off from learning after their initial education. Indeed, the 'know-it-all' mentality is possibly the most fatal condition to have within an organisation in terms of its success and longevity.

This book, then, is about helping you become a better coach by helping others, by unlocking performance through learning and development processes and by at all times stressing the need for personal commitment. Be the change, in fact, you want to see in others. If you are not developing as a person, as a human being, how really will you coach others? You may have all the techniques and tools in the coaching world, but people are quick to spot inauthenticity and the 'going through the motions' type of coaching that is indicative of those who have lost their own passion to self-improve. This book therefore is written in order to help your personal development as you advance through the book; in other words, to self-coach.

But, you may say, there are loads of books on the market about coaching, why should I buy and read this one? What is different about *Mapping Motivation for*

Coaching? The answer to this question is profound and it touches upon a limitation in MacLennan's definition, as fine as that definition is. For the limitation in the definition is not confined to MacLennan alone; no. It is the invisible factor, the thing assumed but which comes after we have dealt with the other stuff, and it's not just about its invisibility with coaching: it's invisible in all the major people disciplines: management, leadership, performance, HR, engagement, recruitment and we could go on. What are we talking about?

First, let's be clear, MacLennan does a fine job subsequently in his book of talking about this issue and has many good ideas about it. But as his definition shows this particular point is invisible – it's not core to the process – it's not at the heart of the process; we may bring it in later, talk about it later, but later, in our view, is too late. What is this issue, this point, this invisible aspect of coaching that is so important and so profound? Of course, if you have read the title of this book you will soon realise the word is motivation. Motivation is the key.

It is true: only *you* can motivate you. And it is also true that most of the motivation that stems from 'Ra-Ra' activities, artificially engineered by HR, O&D, and managers generally – activities such as listening to a motivational speaker, fire-walking, engaging in team physical activities – usually lasts about a fortnight. There's a short-term feel-good factor, and then back at work the excitement and adrenalin rush seem a distant dream, and the old boredoms kick in!

However, the creation of the Motivational Maps has changed this situation, we hope, forever. For the Motivational Maps have now provided a language and metrics in which motivation can be described, measured, monitored and maximised, and the invisible feelings and desires and aversions of the individual (and team and organisation) can be brought to the surface quickly, accurately, and usefully in, basically, 10 minutes!

In short, the invisible energy of motivation can now be made visible and clear. The implications of this for coaching, then, are very deep indeed. MacLennan did not have this technology when he wrote his magisterial book; but we have it now and so it's time to explore how this changes everything and leads to a new model of coaching that builds on and yet supersedes the models that went before.

One anecdotal point to make here would be this: we ourselves as coaches can emphatically state that what before in a coaching session might take the whole (often 90 minutes) of the first coaching session to establish, namely, what is the real issue being presented, can now – with the Motivational Map being completed in advance – be discovered within 20 minutes. And discovered too more accurately, more precisely, and with a greater commitment to the revelations on the part of the client, since often the Map validates what the client is reluctant to admit, but such is its power that it almost becomes a confession. And, lest this be thought: 'well, we would say that wouldn't we?' we can also report that in our system of 'Mappers' (over 400 in 14 countries) and clients (an even great number), we have been told time and time again just how direct and effective the Maps make the coaching process.

This book, then, is your handbook to enable you to become a more effective coach, and you will find, once you master its contents, that it is a resource for life and for all situations. For although our primary concern in writing the book is for professional coaches, organisational managers and leaders to develop their knowledge and skill sets further, the truth is that coaching as a process can be useful in virtually all the important areas of our life. Essentially, coaching is an advanced interpersonal skill and its deployment by you is going to make you a lot more popular and effective whether with your own family and friends, or simply casual acquaintances.

Why? Because a primary requirement of human beings is to be loved. The most effective way to love somebody is to listen to them – not just to hear what they are saying, but to listen with your whole being. As the Egyptian Ptahhotep[7] said 4000 years ago: "To listen is better than anything, thus is born perfect love". And strangely, paradoxically, although effective listening involves silence and spaces, it also involves speaking: asking really good questions. Yes, the kind of thing that coaching perfects in us!

Our intention therefore is to help inform and lead you with coaching practices and principles that invariably deliver results for clients, but also that generate in you a thirst for continuing your own personal development journey. Moreover, perhaps more importantly than anything else, we intend to take you on a journey that allows you to experience the benefit of these principles; principles that help lead people out of doubt, confusion, apathy and fear (the great enemies of achievement and success in life) towards greater clarity, confidence, personal power, and peace of mind. And for the record, incidentally, peace of mind is the ultimate benefit that all human beings want, for it is the goal of all our strivings; as one great religious leader put it, what does it profit to gain the whole world and lose one's soul? Peace of mind is that state in which we are truly content because we have – at last – found our real selves (our soul if you will) and we can rest finally in that bliss of authenticity. As the psychotherapist James Hollis expressed this: "The gods want us to grow up, to step up to that high calling that each soul carries as its destiny".[8]

Prepare yourselves for a journey, then, that is going to take you through a smorgasbord of great ideas, deep knowledge, key skills, powerful principles, practical tips, real case studies, useful references and further resources for you to tap into.

The focus of this book is about the individual, not the team[9] or the whole organisation, because as we have said, coaching is a one-to-one process. Naturally, it should come as no surprise that the effect of coaching on *one person only* can have an inordinate impact on a team and even on a whole organisation. If we keep in mind that profound observation of Peter Drucker,[10] the twentieth century's greatest management consultant, that "Whenever anything is being accomplished, it is being done, I have learned, by a monomaniac with a mission" then the power of the one should be evident. And if the importance of resolving to develop yourself were in doubt, then let's remember the words of Abraham Lincoln: "Always bear in mind that your own determination to succeed is more important than any other one thing".[11] Notice that phrase 'any other one thing': determination alone is not always sufficient to guarantee success, but of all the factors that lead to it, it is certainly the most important. So please, commit to the process.

This book is topographical and so it can be dipped into, especially after it has first been read in its entirety; thus, it may become an easy reference volume. However, just as through practice – your practice – coaching develops, so too is the understanding of motivation and the human psyche cumulative. It was Socrates, amongst others, who insisted that the beginning of wisdom was to know oneself. All personal development must start at that point, including the personal development of the coach. The greatest people who have ever lived have all been people who relentlessly pursued self-knowledge as a primary focus: most people when they start their quest begin with a self-knowledge that may be compared with a reality the size of an anthill. The anthill is busy but does not reflect in any way the true scope of the self. But, as one really begins to understand one's self, a vista opens up and the truly great realise that they are standing somewhere in the Himalayan Mountains! That is a tremendous vision; but even if we don't quite get that far, it would still be significant to at least reach the peaks of the Lake District in Cumbria, for that would be a massive increase on the anthill!

Finally, as part of our commitment to you to make this book your personal journey of discovery we have provided you with a unique opportunity to complete your own Motivational Map. Follow the instructions at the end of this Introduction in the endnote.[12]

Once completed, you will receive a full 15-page client report showing your Motivational Map, what motivates you in your work, in what order and intensity. Shortly afterwards you will also receive a 1-page summary of your report. This is the coaching report, not generally made available, but which explains not only what drives you in your career but also how you are currently feeling about your work and whether it is meeting your needs and your drivers. This can open up a whole new vista for you as to what the issues in your life are. Plus, in conjunction with a qualified Licensed Practitioner (Coach) of motivational mapping, we can see at a glance:

A) Where your career is not fulfilling your needs currently and be able to probe appropriately;
B) How your motivational drivers are likely to evolve naturally over time and compare those with your goal and career plans;
C) Where you may struggle to relate to other drivers either as a manager, leader or colleague.

So without further ado we recommend that you go and complete your Motivational Map before continuing further. You can read this book academically and it will provide useful and insightful information, but the full impact comes if you treat it as a workbook for your own development and absorb the material.

Notes

1 'Executive Coaching as a Transfer of Training Tool: Effects on Productivity in a Public Agency', Gerald Olivero, K. Denise Bane, and Richard F. Kopelman, *Public Personnel Management*, Volume 26.4 (1997).

2 "The International Coach Federation, which has a membership of close to 50,000 professionals, estimates the global coaching sector generates about $2bn a year in revenue" - Maxine Boersma, 'Coaching No Longer the Preserve of Executives', Financial Times, 26/2/2016.

3 Though interestingly, in the eighteenth century, Lord Chesterfield did note one exception to this general rule: "I am very sure that any man of common understanding may, by culture, care, attention, and labor, make himself whatever he pleases, except a great poet".

4 There are almost too many examples to cite of this, and in America it is almost an obligatory mantra - certainly Edison being a patron saint of these kind of admissions. More recently, the world famous sportsman, Michael Jordan said: "I have failed over and over again in my life. And that is why I succeed" - cited in *Forbes* and *The Week*, 10/6/2017.

5 The GROW model is the most well-known of these mainly acronymic processes, which include the SUCCESS, STEPPE, WHAT, FUEL models etc. GROW stands for Goals, Reality (current), Options, Will (or Way forward). These provide useful steps in which the coach can frame a conversation with the client and be sure they are moving them forward. Max Landsberg's popular book, *The Tao of Coaching*, HarperCollins, (1996), is a good example and advocate of the GROW model.

6 *Coaching and Mentoring*, Nigel MacLennan, Gower (1996).

7 Christian Jacq, *The Living Wisdom of Ancient Egypt*, Simon & Schuster (1999).

8 *Finding Meaning in the Second Half of Life*, James Hollis, Gotham/Penguin (2006).

9 Two subsequent books in this series, *Mapping Motivation for Management*, and *Mapping Motivation for Strategy*, will cover team and organisational applications, respectively.

10 "The single-minded ones, the monomaniacs, are the only true achievers. The rest, the ones like me, may have more fun; but they fritter themselves away.... Whenever anything is being accomplished, it is being done, I have learned, by a monomaniac with a mission." - Peter Drucker, *Adventures of a Bystander*, Transaction Publishers (1994).

11 Abraham Lincoln, Letter to Isham Reavis, Nov 5, 1855.

12 To obtain a link to do a Motivational Map, send an email to info@motivationalmaps.com and put the word COACHMAP in the heading.

Summary of Motivational Maps
What you need to know in a nutshell!

Within each person there are nine motivators – we all have these motivators, and we all have the full nine. The difference is that each individual has the nine in a different order and at a different level of intensity. This gives rise to the possibility of millions of potential combinations in an individual's profile. Over 30,000 Maps have been completed and we still have never seen two individuals with identical Maps; furthermore, because motivation is partially based on our belief systems, it changes over time. It is not static or fixed, and so it is impossible to stereotype anyone according to their motivators, since these will change. Usually, most people are directly influenced not by just their top motivator, but by their top three motivators; rarely, this can be their top two or top four, but the scoring shows what really counts or not (which are motivators scoring > 20).

Motivation is energy; it is what fuels us to do 'things' – things we want to do. Without motivation we are unlikely to set out in the direction we want to go (towards our goals) and are even more unlikely to use our knowledge and skills effectively. In short, motivation is the fuel in the tank of the car we call performance. Thus, knowing what motivates us and how to reward – or re-fuel – our motivators is to enable higher levels of energy, greater levels of performance and productivity and to seriously increase our satisfaction with life.

The nine motivators are not random or discrete but instead form a holistic unity. They are divided into three groups of three; the groups like the motivators themselves have properties as well as motivational qualities. Some motivators are aligned and reinforce each other; other motivators conflict and cause tension, whether that be at an individual (that is, internal), team or organisational level. The tension is not necessarily a bad thing; it can lead, for example, to procrastination – to taking longer to make a decision – but equally taking longer can sometimes mean making a better decision. In Motivational Maps, therefore, as an absolute rule, there is no good or bad profile: context determines the meaning of every profile.

So, to expand and summarise the key principles underpinning Motivational Maps, then there are nine key points:

1   All Map profiles are good. There are not good or bad profiles – the diagnostic is ipsative, which means that you are measuring yourself against yourself, so you cannot be 'wrong'. What you 'think' can be wrong but how you 'feel' cannot be: it is how you feel and so it is with your motivators, as they are feeling-based.

2   Context is everything in interpreting Maps. There can be no one meaning isolated from the context in which the individual is operating. Profiles may suit or re-inforce a specific context or not; 'or not' may mean that intention (will power), knowledge, and skill will have to accomplish that which one is not motivated to do, or it can mean the difference between focus (the motivators aligned and not closely scored) and balance (the motivators less aligned and the scoring narrowing or close) and which is relevant in a given situation.

3   Motivational Maps describe, measure, and monitor motivation. They make our invisible emotional drives visible and quantifiable. At last individuals, managers and organisations can get a handle on this key issue and through Reward Strategies do something about it – namely, increase it. Maps are a complete language and metric of motivation.

4   Motivators change over time. This happens because our beliefs change over time and these belief changes affect how we feel and therefore what motivates us. Thus, regular monitoring of motivation is appropriate and effective. From a coaching perspective this is so powerful because it is a focused opportunity to explore, too, what one's beliefs are and whether they are supportive of what one is trying to achieve.

5   Motivational Maps are not a psychometric instrument. Psychometric-type tools inevitably describe a 'fixed' personality, a core which is unchanging. Maps are stable but fluid over time. Maps take an 'energy snapshot', for motivation is energy. Technically, Motivational Maps are a Self-Perception Inventory.

6   Motivational Maps do not and cannot stereotype individuals. This follows from the fact they change over time, so whatever someone's profile is today, there is no guarantee it will be the same tomorrow. That said, the Maps are usually stable for about 18–24 months. But nobody should suggest, in a personality sort-of-way, 'I'm a Searcher' or any other motivator.

7   There are nine motivators but they are correlated into three groups. These three groups represent, amongst other things, the three primary modes of human perception: Feeling, Thinking, and Knowing. Each perception has fascinating and differing properties.

8   Motivation is highly correlated with performance. It is possible to be a high performer and yet de-motivated, but the price for this, middle or long-term, is stress and health problems. Having a highly motivated workforce is going to reduce illness and absenteeism, as well as presenteeism (the being there in body but not in mind or spirit).

9   Motivation is a feature and people buy benefits. Let's not forget that because motivation is a feature, then it features in many core organisational (and non-organisational) activities: leadership, teams, performance, productivity, sales, appraisal, engagement (70 per cent of engagement is motivation), recruitment, careers and more beside. People usually, therefore, buy the effect or benefit of motivation rather than wanting it directly. Think essential oils! Usually applying an essential oil to the skin requires a 'carrier' oil, so too with motivation: it's wrapping the mapping.

What, then, are the nine motivators and what do they mean? The motivators are in an ordered sequence which correlates with Maslow's Hierarchy of Needs (see Figure S.1). At the base are what we call the Relationship (R) motivators – representing the desire for security (the Defender), belonging (the Friend), and recognition (the Star). They are Relationship motivators because the primary concern of all three is people orientation.

Then, in sequence we have the three Achievement (A) motivators. These are in the middle of the hierarchy. First, there is the desire for control (the Director), then the desire for money (the Builder), and finally the desire for expertise (the Expert). They are Achievement motivators because the primary concern of all three is work orientation.

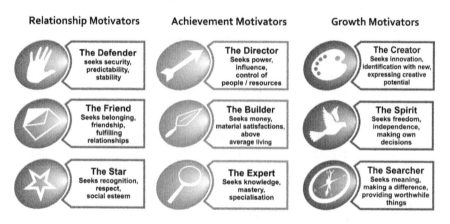

Figure S.1 The nine motivators

Finally, we have the three Growth (G) motivators. These are at the top of the hierarchy. These are the desire for innovation (the Creator), then the desire for autonomy (the Spirit), and at the apex – though this does not imply superiority – we have the desire for meaning or purpose (the Searcher). They are Growth motivators because the primary concern of all three is self-orientation.

From this brief re-cap of what Motivational Maps is about we hope that – if you haven't yet encountered them directly – your first response will be: 'That's fascinating – so what is my profile? What are my top three motivators?' A good idea at this point is to request to do a Motivational Map – see note 12 of the Introduction to find out how to access a Map.

1   Coaching questions

Underpinning coaching, and great coaching especially, is the issue of asking useful, relevant, and sometimes intuitive questions. In later chapters we consider in more detail other core skills that make up the tool-kit, as it were, of the effective coach. But keep in mind that it is not the function of the coach to provide answers for the client – mentors[1] may do that – however, coaches enable the client to find the answers for themselves. In fact, the coach is always acting as a mirror to the client, reflecting back to the client what they have just said because:

a   In the pause between saying what the client says and the coach re-stating it – reflecting it – back to the client, the client's own deeper mind, their subconscious mind, has more chance of kicking in and providing a new insight that had not occurred before;

b   And in the re-statement the perceptive coach has a chance to not only re-state what has been said but also to draw out its true significance. Re-statement is not always exactly the right term for what the coach is doing; paraphrasing would perhaps be more correct. The essence of paraphrase is summarising the essential aspects of what is said;

c   By reflecting the issue back to the source, the client is hearing it again, though with a slightly enhanced or nuanced emphasis (where the coach is being effective) and what this does is reinforce the client's personal ownership of the issue. This increased ownership intensifies the desire to solve the problem[2] – it motivates.

People want to use a coach because they have an 'issue' or a 'problem'; in a perfect world they would not need a coach since they would know what to do. But it mustn't be thought that coaching is for 'problem' people; on the contrary, coaching is possibly the number one technique (alongside its cousin, mentoring) for enhancing just about anybody's performance. Recent research in business indicates that coaching has dramatic effects on performance outcomes[3] and this sort of effect is felt in all areas of coaching. Thus coaching, as has emerged over the last 20 years in the Western world, is a standard process that can help not only the performance of individuals and the productivity of organisations, but also anybody and everybody in facing the 'issues' they have in their private and personal lives. These range from improving health and fitness, raising the level of sporting achievements, coping with relationship, emotional and stress issues, and helping break addictive tendencies.

What, then, can we say coaching is? In the Introduction we cited Professor Nigel MacLennan's powerful definition and its limitation. Expanding it, we derive our own view of coaching:

> *Coaching is a planned intervention(s) by one person (the coach) for another (the client) in which the central purpose is either to motivate, enable and improve the performance of the client in a specific area or for a particular task, or similarly to motivate, enable and improve their capacity for sustained and progressive personal development.*

Clearly, as we explained in the Introduction, there are two purposes of coaching here: for performance and for development. Performance coaching is highly specific, whereas coaching for development, or what might better be called developmental coaching, is more general and of wider import. The former is more results driven, and the latter more process; the former is more about achievement within a role, and the latter more about actualising potential and bringing out latent capabilities. The former, then, in one sense is easier; but the latter is more – to use a Lord of the Rings' word – 'tricksy', though deeply rewarding when done effectively, for both client and coach.

It is worth mentioning here the two continuums of coaching along which all of its skills ultimately derive.[4] The perfect coach would be entirely balanced, but nobody is perfect and so we all have our predilections, or biases, that can give us greater strengths in some areas but less in others.

These continuums or elements are the fact that the coach, on the one hand, has to tread a fine line between supporting their client and challenging them (see Figure 1.1). If they become too supportive – too friendly as it were – they may fail to challenge them sufficiently. But if they challenge them too much without providing adequate support, like some oppressive parent or manager, they may set them up to fail because the challenge is too much. Like yin and yang, then, the coach has to have a balance between these two elements and find the right approach at the right time.

support   challenge

Figure 1.1 Support versus challenge

ACTIVITY 1.1

Analyse your own style of coaching or, if you are not a coach, then of helping people. Do you tend to be more supportive or more challenging? Do you tend to say, 'How can I help you?' (supportive) or do you say 'How are you going to do this?' (challenging)? What are the implications of this for your practice? How do your clients or friends react to your approach to their issues? On reflection, what could be done better or differently in future?

empathy   objectivity

Figure 1.2 Empathy versus objectivity

And, on the other hand, we also have the two related elements of empathy and objectivity (see Figure 1.2). It is important that we practise empathy in order to fully understand the client's position; just understanding it in an intellectual way is invariably to misunderstand it. When we empathise we effectively 'walk in their shoes', so that we can feel the problem as well as cognitively recognising it. But the danger in feeling it as well is that we too get caught up in it and become unable to see the wood for the trees. The antidote to this is being objective; in other words, seeing the reality for what it really is. This is an important quality, but taken too far we treat the client as an accountant would treat the numbers in our business: routinely, matter-of-factly, and without any real regard for what is truly driving behaviours – our motivators in fact. This, too, can be fatal to successful coaching.

ACTIVITY 1.2

Again, review your own style of coaching or even of helping people. Do you tend to be more empathic or more objective? Do you tend to say, 'How do you feel?' (empathic) or do you say 'What happened when …?' (objective)? What are the implications of this for your practice? How do your clients or friends react to your approach to their issues? On reflection, what could be modified or improved in your approach? And ask yourself this: do you feel any of your client's emotions, or remain detached when working with them?

If we now combine these two elements into one graph (see Figure 1.3), we find there are four dominant options that present themselves.

These titles – Motivator, Goal-setter, Friend, and Observer – are four important 'roles' that the coach plays within the process of coaching. Each coach will be different, and with a different emphasis, but to coach at all effectively they will have to negotiate between all of these roles if they are to be effective; and they will need to be careful that none of the four roles becomes a chronic weakness which lets down the effectiveness of the other strong areas. Challenging without support is destined to fail; empathy without objectivity is bound to be blind; support without challenge is bound to underperform; and objectivity without empathy will lead to revulsion. Finally, it may well be that the great coach uses these four dimensions rather like a master pianist might use certain notes on a piano – depending on the audience (the client), certain elements might be more appropriate at any given moment in the client's developmental cycle. In practice, as the client–coach

Figure 1.3 Four dimensions of coaching

relationship deepens, there is often a movement from being supportive and empathetic towards being more challenging and objective.

ACTIVITY 1.3

Study the scales in Figure 1.4 and give yourself a score out of 10 in each of the four dimensions. A score of 1 means that you barely have that element whereas a 10 indicates that you have a superabundance of it. Do this quickly and without too much premeditation. Once you have done it, look at your scores. Which of the four roles do you think is your particular strength – Motivator, Goal-setter, Friend, or Observer? Which is your weakest link? How does this process of reflection help inform the development of your coaching in the future and with which friends/colleagues/clients?

At this point it is good to introduce the relevance of all this to Motivational Maps[5] and the nine motivators that drive human behaviour. The nine motivators are: Searcher (making a difference), Spirit (being free), Creator (wanting innovation), Expert (liking learning), Builder (wanting material rewards), Director (practising control), Star (wanting status), Friend (wanting to belong), and Defender (needing security). Each of these can be allocated into one of the four dimensions of coaching, except perhaps Expert, since learning can inform all four areas. With that in mind, then:

Figure 1.4 Scoring your four dimensions

ACTIVITY 1.4

Consider Figure 1.5 and ask yourself, if Expert is common to all four elements, where do the other eight motivators most likely sit? We say most likely because there can be some leeway here, as we will explain (see Figure 1.5).

Four things at least to notice here:

a   First, the more Relationship type motivators – Friend, Star, and Defender – tend to occupy the more Supportive end of the spectrum, which seems entirely reasonable, given their preoccupation with other people.

b   Conversely, the more Growth oriented motivators – Creator, Spirit, and Searcher – tend to be more preoccupied with the challenges, because the challenge (and challenges are invariably about the future) will be perceived by them as making the biggest difference.

c   Third, this allocation is the ideal scenario and in certain (often many) situations one of the Map motivators may well occupy a different quadrant than shown in Figure 1.5. A good example might be the Director motivator. Ideally, given Director in their profile, we want coaches who are objective and supportive, but we can easily find them objective and challenging. However, too challenging combined with too much objectivity can be perceived as pushy and mechanical.

d   Finally, if you have done a Map and you know your top three motivators, do they tend to corroborate your own assessment of your quadrant strength from Activity 1.3? It is not a cause for concern if they do not; what you are trying to establish – from a variety of perspectives – is what your core strengths are as a coach and where maybe some more work and expertise needs to be developed. And – especially if Expert is your lowest motivator[6]! – one needs to doubly commit to improving the weaker element. Often very experienced coaches will have awareness of their natural default setting and over time

Figure 1.5 Maps and the four dimensions

will have developed their weaknesses to a point whereby, say, the naturally challenging and objective coach is also seen as friendly and supportive (this is an ideal scenario). What we want to help to develop are coaches with that awareness.

If we now consider the core skills that emerge from this overview of the elements of coaching, then it may become apparent that two skills in particular emerge as a result of reflecting on (empathy and support) and (challenge and objectivity).

ACTIVITY 1.5

What are these two core skills of coaching? Before we go further, write down what you think these two core skills are.

It would be nice to think, as so many managers and businesses do, that setting goals is all that is necessary to achieve high performance levels. Goal-setting has a vital role to play and as we can see is one of the four dimensions. But, if we want to get the best from people – from our client, friends, and family members (including our children) – the first thing to do, long before setting a goal for them, is to build rapport,[7] which addresses the empathy and support dimensions. Without rapport, the chances of being effective as a coach are extremely limited. The second core skill, addressing the challenge and objectivity elements, is questioning; and questioning here most emphatically includes the sub-skill, which can almost become a stand-alone and separate skill, of listening. As we will see, Motivational Maps has a lot to add to our understanding and our performance in these areas.

Typically, understanding how to build rapport with another person involves what might be called a combination of sub-skills and attitudes. However, one should be under no illusions: despite the proliferation of books[8] promising to enable you to get on with anybody, anywhere, within ten minutes if you just follow their process, creating rapport with another person is not easy and is fraught with problems – it requires understanding of what influences rapport. Before introducing Motivational Maps as a targeted help in this arena, what usually counts towards building rapport?

In building rapport it is useful to think of a three-step process[9]: knowing you, liking you, and, finally, trusting you. This is as true in coaching as it is in sales for, ultimately, we are all into selling our ability to influence others.

ACTIVITY 1.6

Are you conscious of building rapport, especially when you meet new people or when working with a client? How do you build rapport? What steps do you take?

Knowing you

Start with the body: smile, introduce yourself and what you do, and then thank them for their time in speaking with you. That sets a scene for 'knowing you'. Clearly, how you introduce yourself is critical: not only has one to avoid overloading people with 'me' statements and assertions designed to inflate one's own importance but, more significantly, you need to be able to excite curiosity about you and what you do or enable them to see how talking to you will benefit them. The principles of physically meeting somebody so that one can say one 'knows' them are also true online: we create a persona online and this too needs to be welcoming, warm, and more about the client than the self.

Liking you

For the client, there are five 'triggers' that can encourage them to like you. (1) Physical attractiveness, or what has been called the halo effect.[10] We impute other virtues – mental, emotional, moral – to people we perceive as attractive. Attractiveness, however, is not something 'fixed', or that we are simply born with (or not!). Hence the importance of clothes, grooming, and conscious image-management. (2) Similarity or likeness: we tend to like people more if we perceive they are like us. Some aspects of this – where we were born or educated – may be beyond our control, but things such as body language, voice tone, and dress are quite malleable. (3) People like us more when we compliment them; not crudely, and not flattery, but when we genuinely notice and express appreciation for some aspect of them, their possessions, achievements or qualities. (4) We increase our likeability when we are familiar to the other person. Familiarity occurs when they are exposed to us and our name more frequently – through repetition, through co-operation; and when we think about it, this is exactly how we form friends: by spending more time in their company. And, to extend this further, it may be because they have read about us, or seen our website or blogs, and so on. (5) We get to like others more if we can associate them with good experiences. This good experience may be physical (we play golf together), intellectual (you make me think in new ways), or emotional (I find you very supportive). But ultimately, we all prefer to be with people who give us good experiences, and these can be very simple things such as providing a good quality cup of coffee or tea when they visit you!

ACTIVITY 1.7

Which of these five triggers do you typically, whether consciously or otherwise, use to build rapport with people? Which, perhaps, might you use more of? How do you intend to improve your ability to build rapport over the next 12 months?

Trusting you

So, they know you, they like you, and critically to build true rapport they must trust you. All serious relationships are based on trust, and without trust no serious work or business (or relationship) can be carried out or function. The coach, then, must engender trust in the client. Trust builds over time; for everyone, until full trust is established, is always asking themselves, 'Can I trust this person? Can I trust what they are saying to me? Is there some secret agenda?'

Trust comes about when we are consistent – we practise what we preach, we walk the talk, and we do what we say we are going to do on a repeated basis. Trust also comes about from first impressions: so, we return to how we appear and especially critical are our body language and eye contact. It is not a coincidence that in the English language we have words like 'shifty', which indicate somebody is not to be trusted. This is because people intuitively pick up on the fact that the body and the words are not consonant.

But finally, here, we come full circle, for the last and perhaps critical aspect of building trust – hence building rapport – leads directly on to our second core skill:

questioning and listening. The listening component of the questioning skill is central to trust. Real listening is effectively an act of love.[11] Nearly everyone experiences the sense that nobody is listening to them or taking them seriously; we all want to demand attention – and as children we get some from our parents, but probably not enough; and then from friends and teachers, but invariably we wonder, 'Is anyone really listening?'[12] Falling in love and having a partner is really that throw of the dice whereby we commit to someone – that special someone – who if nobody else does, is the one person who will listen to us. Of course, when that fails, it is extremely distressing and debilitating for the individual. They talk about 'falling out of love', but almost always, before they fell out of love, they were no longer listening.

Let us then examine some of the questions and listening skills that Maps help us develop. First, in Neuro Linguistic Programming (also see Chapter 4) – or NLP – there is a concept called pacing in which we need to *match* or *mirror* the behaviour (including their *behaviour* – or style – with language!) of the person we are seeking to influence. It's important that we don't attempt to do this mechanically, but from the heart; in a way when we 'pace' another person we are giving them more space to be themselves, as well as putting our own position in the best possible light in terms of their interpretation of it.

If we keep in mind this pacing concept, then there are three major, generic areas (apart from motivational specifics) in which the Maps can help us interpret what the client is thinking and feeling. These three areas are: attitude to risk and change, likely speed of decision making, and preferred learning style (see Figure 1.6). If we think about building rapport, it should be manifest that if we accommodate the client's taste for risk/change, move at their speed in decision making, and talk to them in their learning style, our chances of building rapport are greatly enhanced.

In terms of what this means for building rapport, consider the following: your Motivational Map contains a RAG score[13] and this indicates whether you – or your client – are dominantly Relationship, Achievement, or Growth oriented. In dealing with a client it is almost always easier to build rapport with someone whose Map profile is like one's own as then you will naturally adopt the same sort of attitude to risk/change (RC), decision-making (DM), and learning style (LS) as the client. There will be, in short, a resonant sympathy. But, of course, in many instances the client will have a very different, even opposite profile, from yourself.

Hence, it is worth thinking through how one can adapt one's own style to more suitably match that of the client's.

If the client is R (Relationship) dominant in their motivators, then it is important to:

Minimise risks involved	(RC)
Consider only essential change	(RC)
Propose small steps not big leaps	(RC)
Give plenty of time for the client to consider options	(DM)
Go slow	(DM)
Provide plenty of evidence	(DM)
Be process and systems focused	(LS)
Show images of the processes working	(LS)

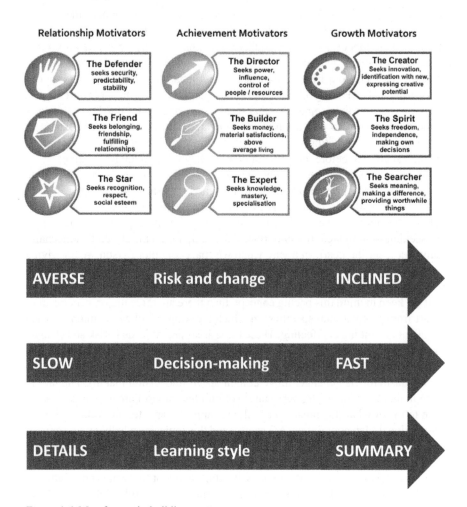

Figure 1.6 Map factors in building rapport

Tell stories of others for whom this has worked	(LS)
Consider the people involved and their reactions	(LS)
Give guarantees	(RC)

Remember you have to address their mind-set which says: 'This is how I/we do things here – why not, or why would we not do things this way?' Be expert and deferential; focus essentially on people.

If the client is A (Achievement) dominant in their motivators, then it is important to:

Talk of calculated risks/rewards	(RC)
Consider only necessary changes	(RC)
Propose sufficient, decisive steps with controlled timetable	(RC)

Go steady	(DM)
Provide plenty of supportive numbers and facts	(DM)
Be outcome oriented	(DM)
Show what results arise from these proposed actions	(LS)
Show what advantages to the bottom line	(LS)
Consider resources involved and how they will be deployed	(DM)
Feed their competitiveness	(LS)
Reassure them that they are in control	(DM)

Remember you have to address their mind-set which says: 'How do I/we achieve this?' Be effective and goal-driven; focus essentially on things.

If the client is G (Growth) dominant in their motivators, then it is important to:

Ensure proposals are exciting	(RC)
Accept no risk, no reward	(RC)
Talk importance, big ideas, wider scheme of things	(LS)
Consider substantial changes and bold move	(RC)
Propose radical, transformational initiatives that have long shelf-life	(RC)
Go fast	(DM)
Stress 'the difference', uniqueness and the big deal	(DM)
Be intuitive and holistic	(LS)
Avoid overmuch detail	(LS)
Always keep the big picture in forefront of their thinking	(LS)
Enable them to see personal growth benefits clearly	(LS)

Remember you have to address their mind-set which says: 'What will I/we be in five years' time?' Be experimental and envisioning; focus essentially on ideas.

Keep in mind that some individuals may be so closely scored in their RAG that one will have to adapt aspects of more than one preference. Also, keep in mind, that individuals who are closely scored (a range of no more than 4 points from the top to the bottom) may well experience tension and indecisiveness in deciding what they want since their motivators are conflicting.

ACTIVITY 1.8

At this point, knowing your own Map RAG scores, it would be useful for you to consider, which is your dominant – R or A or G? First, do the above descriptors adequately match your experience of how you approach the three Map factors? Secondly, given you know the Map profile of the client in advance of the meeting to coach them, what do you intend to do to enable you to 'match' or pace their style?

Once we have built rapport, we need to ask good questions and listen carefully to the responses in order to help the client. What are good questions to ask the client?

Typically, coaching has its own set of questions that can be asked. Different schools of coaching have different emphases here. Michael Bungay Stanier[14] in his excellent book, *The Coaching Habit*, lists seven questions that, he claims, can unpack most issues from most people. These are highly effective and well explained but at an even profounder level are the 'change talk' questions used by Miller and Rollnick in their classic book, *Motivational Interviewing*.[15] Here we have a process which involves presenting the client with subtle questions surrounding four key issues: the disadvantages of the status quo, the advantages of change, creating optimism for change, and enabling an intention to change.[16] So, on the one hand, then, we have seven simple questions and we can immediately get stuck in, as it were; whereas, on the other, we have an in-depth psychological approach based on very serious and detailed research, but that requires a large commitment of time and training to acquire. Both have advantages and downsides, and no one approach can be considered definitive. Why? Because we are dealing with people. Indeed, as both approaches recognise,[17] it is not enough to have a checklist of questions that are asked mechanically; the effective coach has to respond to client answers and veer a course appropriately. And that course may not be in the direction that they (the client and/or the coach) originally anticipated.

How, then, does doing a Motivational Map help with the coaching process of asking the client questions? First, the advantage of doing the Map is that the initial conversation can focus on it and not immediately on the issues of the client. This is important because it takes away the client's potential apprehension and it directs attention towards the objective 'thing' that they have completed – the Map. Whether or not the results of the Map have been released in advance to the client, once the profile has been fed back, a series of questions become inevitable, and relatively easier to answer.

ACTIVITY 1.9

If you have or had done a Map, what questions might you expect somebody to ask of you about it?

Asked casually, the first question might be: *How did you find the Map?* Notice how general and non-committal this is. It appears to be a 'thinking' question, but whenever you ask someone how they find something we are really inviting them to talk about how they feel. You can't be 'wrong' in how you find something because it's how you feel about it. In the course of the client's answers about how they 'found' it any number of issues can surface. For example, to the bland response, 'Interesting', the follow-up sub-question must be, 'How so?' or 'In what way?' Most responses, however, are not bland, but more 'a-ha'.

Second, you ask, *How accurate is the Map?* Notice here too that we are not saying that the Map is accurate, but that the client be the judge of its accuracy. But from the coaching perspective this is vital – for either way, accurate or not, it enables the coach to assess where the client is emotionally and energetically. Most people – that is, some 95 per cent[18] of them – find the Map extremely accurate. That confirmation is vital information on which to go to work. Remember: if it is accurate (and if it is not, then they will explain why it is not, thus revealing more about themselves), then you have a detailed emotional and energetic snapshot of where they currently are, and based on only two questions! And why is this important? Because if we know the emotional and energetic state of the client we can be highly sensitive to likely issues and challenges that arise from it; furthermore, we can begin that process of diagnosis and prescription long before we have even finished our examination of their 'condition'. Any example would do here, but, say, they confirm that Searcher, the desire to make a difference, is indeed their number one motivator and that their satisfaction rating is only 4 out 10. We will therefore know that whatever role they are performing, is either intrinsically meaningless to them, or simply too routine, and that to help them, we as coaches, are going to need to direct them to ways of increasing meaning and of acquiring more quality feedback.

Finally, at this stage, we ask: *What did you learn about yourself?* Notice that this allows the client to share any insights they gleaned from the Map profile. Of course, 'Nothing' is not an answer one wants to hear, but if one does hear it, the best sub-question response probably is: 'So what is the most important thing in the Map profile for you?' We do find people who like (fondly) to imagine that they already know everything about themselves that there is to know, but we have yet to find anybody who does not answer that last question, for there is always something that absorbs their attention in the profile. Why? Because it is about them.

But where are we, then, after these three (sub-questions included) questions? The three core questions are summarised in Figure 1.7:

In asking these three questions we have established:

1   How they *feel* – how they 'found' (out) – about themselves because the Map is a mirror of themselves. It is an ipsative test, which means they are literally comparing their self with their self.[19]
2   How they *think* – accuracy requires thought – about what they feel about themselves!
3   What they *know* – learning requires reflecting (thought) on feeling, leading to knowing at a confirmatory level where we know this to be the case with a deeper level of commitment.

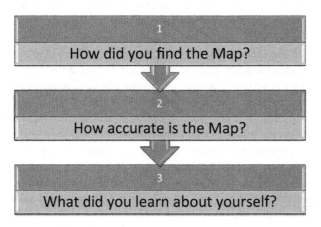

Figure 1.7 Map questions for starters

In short, these three Map-specific questions have established levels of self-awareness and information at the three primary modes of human perception: Feel–Think–Know.[20] This is profoundly rapport building in and of itself. Furthermore, we have gained an insight, as coaches, as to where the client is emotionally and energetically. This is important and precedes goal-setting. For what, truly, is the point in helping people set ambitious goals for themselves when they are either not emotionally clear on what they want, or are in a state of low motivation, or both things simultaneously?

And we know something else too. We know, again as coaches, even if the client is not clear on what he or she wants, we are! Because we know from their Map what they subconsciously desire; that is, the secret questions – the real filters – that they are applying to every idea and proposal and question we put to them. And this is not just with us. In every situation, but especially work, they are asking three key subconscious questions that are correlated with their top three motivators (see Figure 1.8).

If we take the above questions and consider them from the point of view of building rapport, or even more fundamentally as to whether a client wants or accepts a coach (keep in mind that some people select coaches and others have them foisted on them as part of a programme) or not, then the issues in Figure 1.9 would need addressing:

ACTIVITY 1.10

If you have a prospect or client and they have done a Map for you and you know their top three motivators, how would you address the three subconscious questions that arise from Figure 1.9? What ideas would you work into your presentation? What benefits would you stress about what you can do for them? Clearly, if you can answer these questions in advance of a session, then this has big sales implications.

Motivator	Key subconscious question	Key response-solution
DEFENDER	How do I know this will work?	continuity, warranty, peace of mind guarantees
FRIEND	How do I know you'll be there for me?	loyalty, liking, rapport
STAR	How do I know I'll look good?	prestige, importance, being noticed
DIRECTOR	How do I know I'll be in control?	power, control, influence
BUILDER	How do I know I'll make money?	money, possessions, elevation
EXPERT	How do I know I'll be an expert?	know-how, mastery, insight
CREATOR	How do I know I'll be able to make changes?	innovation, latest, advanced
SPIRIT	How do I know I'll be able to prioritise?	freedom, independence, decision-making
SEARCHER	How do I know I'll make a difference?	making a difference, impact, purposeful

Figure 1.8 Nine questions and nine response-solutions

Motivator	Key subconscious question about coaching	?
DEFENDER	How do I know coaching will work for me?	?
FRIEND	How will coaching enable you to like and support me?	?
STAR	How will coaching enhance my reputation?	?
DIRECTOR	How will coaching extend my control and influence?	?
BUILDER	How will coaching make me more money?	?
EXPERT	How will coaching make me more expert in my role?	?
CREATOR	How will coaching help me effect change?	?
SPIRIT	How will coaching free up my time?	?
SEARCHER	How will coaching enable me to make a difference?	?

Figure 1.9 Nine subconscious questions about the coach

Again, keep in mind most individuals will have three of these nine questions jostling in their subconscious, yet they will be in a strict hierarchical order as indicated by the Motivational Map; therefore, the top motivator should be the primary focus. For example, if the top three motivators were Creator, Spirit, and Searcher – in that order – then we can see in Figure 1.10 the hierarchy of the subconscious questions from Creator to Spirit and lastly to Searcher.

It should be clear that this model of coaching doesn't start with what the client's goals might be or what is on their mind. This may be a useful starting point, but it also may lead too quickly into a logical, 'think' type analysis that proves to be premature. No, by considering the motivators and the client's response to them we are immediately thrown into how the client feels as the starting point, and from that there is an increase in their emotional and energetic self-awareness. This is important because it is setting up the client to be emotionally aligned with the actions and goals they are subsequently going to choose; this means there is far more chance that they will invest heavily in doing and achieving them.

What we now want to do in this opening, exploratory stage of the coaching investigation into the client's condition is to further probe how the motivators and the current role match, or not. Of course, we already know partially from the

Figure 1.10 The three subconscious questions we are asking based on our Map

Personal Motivational Audit (PMA) scores how they feel about role satisfaction (see Figure 1.11 for how the numbers are laid out on page 13 of the Motivational Map).[21]

As we can see in Figure 1.11, this particular person has three top motivators – Spirit, Builder and Expert, and in that rank order. We also see that this client is 5/10 satisfied with his current levels of autonomy (Spirit), 8/10 for his levels of money (Builder), but 10/10 for his sense of expertise (Expert). Overall, based on the three PMA scores and the proprietary algorithm used by Motivational Maps, this person is 64 per cent motivated.

Here are some questions to open up the client further.

1 What would be different if you were more motivated in your current role?
2 How important is motivation to you? Out of 10?
3 How can you get more motivated/sustain your motivation at this 10 level?
4 How – exactly – does your current role fulfil your top three motivators? And how does it not fulfil your motivators? What can be changed?
5 What 'rewards' would improve your motivations?
6 What would an increase in motivation do for your performance and productivity in your current role?
7 How can I help you become more motivated?

These questions do not need to be all answered by the client, or necessarily dealt with sequentially. But they are all prompts to a deeper understanding of where the client currently 'is'. And, of course, let us not forget as we end this chapter that these questions can also be used to self-coach. Try them!

Summary

1 Coaches reflect back poignant statements that clients make to help them become aware of what is occurring subconsciously.

Motivator	Score	PMA Score / 10
Spirit	27	5
Builder	26	8
Expert	24	10

Figure 1.11 An example set of PMA scores for top three motivators – as per page 13 of your Motivational Map

2   Coaching is a mix of empathy and objectivity, challenge and support; the greater the rapport the greater your ability to challenge effectively.
3   Building rapport is the first core skill of effective coaching and mirroring is an effective way of building rapport quickly.
4   For a client to become a coaching client they go through a process of knowing, liking and then trusting you.
5   Knowledge and understanding of the Motivational Map can drastically enhance your ability to build rapport, especially its depiction of risk and change, speed of decision-making and learning style.
6   Using a Map as a starting point for coaching conversations provides a simple, easily acceptable and non-threatening way of opening up a coaching conversation or opportunity.
7   Through understanding the client's Map in advance of the meeting you are aware of their subconscious motivational desires!
8   When choosing a coach, the client's motivational drivers play a significant part in their decision-making process.
9   By understanding our client's Map we can have a much greater influence and create action plans which both work for the client and in which they are more greatly invested.

Notes

1 The distinction between a coach and a mentor or between the two processes is subtle and sometimes blurred. Generally it is thought that the mentor tends to be more directive towards, more experienced and knowledgeable than, more senior than, the client; whereas the coach tends to be more exploratory, more outside the immediate domain of the client, and 'more' equal in terms of status.
2 Nigel MacLennan, *Coaching and Mentoring*, Gower (1999). MacLennan puts it this way: "If you own a problem - if that problem is inside you, if it has become part of your soul - finding the energy, commitment and persistence to solve it is easy". For 'energy' we might substitute the word 'motivation'.
3 "Organizations where senior leaders 'very frequently' coach had 21% higher business results." - 2017 from Bersin: http://bit.ly/2sRdMfv; the Ken Blanchard Organisation puts productivity gains from coaching at 57 per cent: http://bit.ly/2tdmP6j.
4 David Clutterbuck and Jenny Sweeney, "Coaching and Mentoring", in *The Gower Handbook of Management* (1998).
5 For information and understanding of Motivational Maps, see James Sale, *Mapping Motivation,* Gower (2016), especially Chapter 3.
6 The relevance of this point is that the desire to learn new stuff and improve is obviously not so strong where that motivator is weakest.
7 MacLennan (ibid.) identifies four keys of coaching: rapport, intuitive questions, goals, and the client taking responsibility for the outcome. These are four big areas and even in self-coaching developing a rapport with oneself, as counter-intuitive as that sounds, is important and not so obvious! We deal with this in more detail in several chapters but especially in Chapters 5 and 6, where we consider barriers to success, and in Chapter 7, where we consider changing our values.

8 Starting almost certainly with the classic, Dale Carnegie, *How to Win Friends and Influence People*, Cedar Press (1953 [1936]), but since then books like, *How to Make Anyone Like You* by Leil Lowndes, HarperCollins (2000), the first section of which is entitled: How to be a People Magnet.

9 Bob Burg puts it this way: "All things being equal, people will do business with and refer business to, those people they know, like and trust." http://bit.ly/2tXf48b.

10 Edward L. Thorndike, "A constant error in psychological ratings", *Journal of Applied Psychology,* 4 (1), (1920).

11 Cited in the Introduction: "To listen is better than anything, thus is born perfect love" - Vizier Ptahhotep, *The Maxims of Good Discourse* (ca. 2200 BCE) - translated Wim van den Dungen (1999).

12 "Everything is going on its own; nobody listens to anybody else - you simply create noise, not music" - Osho, *Intuition*, Saint Martin's Griffin (2002).

13 The Motivational Map is a 15-page report and the RAG scores are included on page 5.

14 Michael Bungay Stanier, *The Coaching Habit*, Box of Crayons Press (2016). The seven questions are: What's on your mind? And what else? What's the real challenge here for you? What do you want? How can I help? If you're saying Yes to this, what are you saying No to? What was most useful for you?

15 William R. Miller and Stephen Rollnick, *Motivational Interviewing: Preparing People for Change*, The Guilford Press (2002).

16 Typical questions here that might kick off all four areas (and there are many others) are, respectively: What worries you about your current situation? How would you like for things to be different? What makes you think that if you did decide to make a change, you could do it? What would you be willing to try?

17 Perhaps the most well-known coaching model of all is the GROW model, which stands for Goals, Reality, Options, and Wrap-up. It is well described in Max Landsberg's book, *The Tao of Coaching,* HarperCollins (1996).

18 Face Validity testing of the Motivational Map indicates that 95 per cent of respondents consider the Map accurate.

19 Ipsative assessment; and not normative (where they compare themselves, or are compared, with others) or criterion-based (where they are compared with a standard).

20 For more on Feel-Think-Know see Chapter 3 of *Mapping Motivation*, James Sale, Gower (2016).

21 For more information on PMA scores, see Chapter 4 of *Mapping Motivation*, James Sale, Gower (2016).

2 Coaching for higher performance

Coaching starts with considering the issue of self-awareness for the simple reason that the person who is not self-aware has – by definition – no awareness, or consciousness, that there is anything on which to work within one self. This applies as much to self-development as it does to coaching a client. If a cat scratches its fur going through a barbed wire fence, we know it has become 'aware' of the injury because it will start to lick the wound relentlessly in its efforts to heal the scratch. So even animals become highly self-aware of the issues that concern them; although in human beings, with their powerful intellects and advanced emotional apparatus, this is a far more complex activity.

Coaching, then, in simplistic terms might be said to be a three-step process:

1 Enabling the client to become more self-aware;
2 Facilitating their decision to change;
3 Helping the client generate actions to support and achieve the change – new rituals and habits.

But what, we may ask, is it that humans become self-aware about? As a starting point we might say, the Self. The Self is the modern psychological term used to describe what in the past we called the soul. What this Self or soul is lies beyond the scope of this book, but one does not need to be specifically religious to resonate with the idea, common all over the world, "that there is some part of us which should not be sold, betrayed or lost at any cost".[1] It is who we are at a root level and one only needs to reflect that everybody – yes, everybody – at some point in their life talks to themselves; indeed, many people do it all the time. But who are we speaking to when we talk to ourselves? It is as if there are two people present in this self-dialogue. The intellect or the mind or the ego perhaps talking to the deeper Self, the soul, and if it waits long enough, getting answers back.

This is a fascinating topic: the human person is one, but already we find 'two' dialoguing within. If we take this a stage further, one clear model that is useful from a coaching perspective is to see a human being as having four interrelated yet distinct strands, rather like four strands in a rope that weave around each other to form one cable and which as a result of the interweaving is immeasurably stronger (see Figure 2.1).

Figure 2.1 The four rope strands of the Self's body, mind, emotion, and spirit

These four strands[2] are: the body (physical – doing), the mind (mental – thinking), the emotions (emotional – feeling), and the spirit (spiritual – knowing/being). Well-being is critical in all four areas, and a prolonged or sustained problem in one area will inevitably spill over and contaminate another. For example, there is now a well-known medical discipline called Psycho-immunology, which is the study of the interaction between psychological processes and the nervous and immune systems of the human body. In other words, 'mere' emotional stress can cause life threatening illnesses in the body. And so it is with all four areas interacting. For the sake of clarity, the spiritual strand is not necessarily about religion or being religious; it is about man's search for meaning.[3] We need only to contemplate that there have been many examples to show how this can affect the whole person – of people who, regrettably, have lost all meaning in their lives, leading to negative thoughts, emotional depressions, and, in some instances, to suicide and thus the death of the body.

Just, then, as weaknesses in any area affect other areas, so too do strengths. And here's where coaching can help. A starting point for self-awareness might be: How resilient are we in each of these four areas or strands of our Self? And having reviewed where we are, then to take action as appropriate. Figure 2.2 provides a simple diagnostic to help you review where you are.

ACTIVITY 2.1

Look at Figure 2.2 and, without agonising over the result, jot down a score out of 10 for each category. So, for example, that you are in tip-top health with no illnesses, then you would be a 10/10; on the other hand, if you have just had a triple-heart bypass, you might score yourself

2/10. Similarly, with all the other seven categories: How do you rate your zest, 10/10 meaning you are really bursting with energy and 1/10 meaning you never stir from watching TV on the couch? Is your thinking clear and are you creative in your thinking? Do you have resolute optimism, expecting things to turn out well, in your emotions, and does kindness predominate in your thinking, especially toward your Self? Or are you bleak and always angry? Finally, are you on a mission that is more important than you are, and does that mission involve serving others at a deeper level? Give your answers out of 10, being max, and 1 being almost entirely not.

When you have done this, take some time to look at your scores. Here are some rough guidelines: scores above 8 are excellent, 6–8 are good, 3–5 are poor, 1–2 are a major challenge. Also note whether there is one area especially that is low and problematic. If so, this is what is sometimes called the 'Choke Point' – the point that is preventing achievement in your other areas or overall. To take a simple example, if all your scores are 9 or 10 but your health is a 2/10, then eventually your health condition will impede your otherwise excellent progress.

This 'excellent progress' that we wish to make, therefore, does involve our own four strands being stronger, more resilient, and more interactive; each strand depends on every other strand for its strength and versatility. For some clients, not being aware that they have an issue in a specific strand can be a revelation; coaching is a mechanism to help them explore these strands and to achieve greater self-awareness. But to be frank, most of the coaching going on in the world does not happen because people want the benefit of self-awareness! Some do, but many want coaching because it leads to that 'excellent progress', which is invariably

PHYSICAL HEALTH	Health	Zest
MENTAL STRENGTH	Clarity	Creativity
EMOTIONAL WELL-BEING	Optimism	Kindness
SPIRITUAL HEALTH	Mission	Service to others

Figure 2.2 Physical, mental, emotional, and spiritual strands of our being

towards the client's goals. We call this 'performance' and performing well. Indeed, all healthy personalities want to perform at a high level, because

a   it feels good and boosts the self-esteem, and
b   because it enables superior results and outcomes in all our endeavours.

Superior results, of course, lead usually to

c   superior rewards!

Hence we need to look at Performance (a process) in some detail. Before we do, however, we would like to share with you a simple coaching tool that we have developed to get to the root of what is causing the client pain or acting as an impediment to future success (an outcome). The model presented in Figure 2.2 is usable but basic. What if we could cover all the bases in one diagnostic? Our work in this field has led us to create a model that expands the basic four strands into seven elements for success (see Figure 2.3).This more expansive model includes features that impact our overall Self such as Quality of Relationships, which can have a huge impact on our emotions and sense of meaning. Furthermore, this model, though still a self-awareness diagnostic, now specifically addresses the issues of performance and success.

ACTIVITY 2.2

Complete Figure 2.3 by scoring out of 10 how you feel about each of the 10 components of the seven success elements. The column, Current Position/Detail, provides some handy pointers as to how to interpret each of the concepts we introduce.

Key factors for development: Take your lowest score and use this as the basis of a development plan that takes at least 18 months to complete! It is a mistake – usually – to think that one can change one's life overnight. Even the profoundest insights and mental shifts require time to be practised and embedded. In Chapter 3 we look in more detail about the Pareto Principle and of Kaisen[4] in coaching methodology. Oftentimes, slow and easy, the tortoise, wins the race.

A rough guide to scoring would be in one of four ranges:

80+ – you are on course for a successful life
60–79 – you have many elements in place, tweaking needed
35–59 – some big changes are needed to get what you want
0–34 – you are very unhappy – resolve to change now!

RELATIONSHIPS ACHIEVEMENT GROWTH	CURRENT POSITION / 10	CURRENT POSITION / DETAIL
1. SELF ESTEEM x 3 Contentment & control (enoughness, less stress)		Do you sleep well? Examine the 5 Hindrances. Do you feel sufficient for most situations you find yourself in?
Confidence (self-efficacy & optimism)		Do you believe in yourself? Do you feel that things are going to work out well for you?
Communication (assertiveness, expression)		Can you say what you feel directly? Can you say no? Do you express yourself?
2. ENERGY x 2 Health		Are you in good physical & mental health?
Zest		How much energy & zest do you have on a day-by-day basis?
3. QUALITY RELATIONSHIPS Sustained, developed		Do you have a substantial network of long-term genuinely loving/caring relationships?
4. WEALTH Increased options		Do you have enough money set aside to stop worrying about money?
5. MEANING Purpose, worthy goals		Do you have a purpose in life? Do you have worthy goals and ideals?
6. GROWTH Realising potential		Are you becoming all you might be? Are you realising your full potential in life?
7. SELF-AWARENESS Reality checks		Do you seek to learn about yourself – through self-analysis and by scrutinising the feedback from others?
TOTAL: %		

Figure 2.3 Seven success elements

*The five Buddhist hindrances are covered in more detail in Chapter 4, but they are: sensual craving, ill will (or hatred), sloth, worry, doubt (or wavering). They are included here because all five are indicative of low esteem.

Keep in mind these scores are not an absolute law. But we have found with hundreds of clients that the four quadrants of scoring do give a pretty accurate picture. This is especially true where the client, perhaps, has scored big in one area – say, wealth – and may be a millionaire, BUT – are they successful? Their relationships may have failed, they cannot relax and their health may be poor; or to put it as GK Chesterton did: "The typical modern man is the insane millionaire, who has drudged to get money, and then finds he cannot enjoy even money, but only drudgery".[5] This cannot be construed as success in life, for apart from the lack of true meaning, there is an underlying unhappiness. The same excess in one or two other elements equally can cause imbalance elsewhere.

We come, then, to discussing the issue of performance. First, we need to reiterate what we said in the introduction: that we all start by performing badly. But we go through a learning and developmental process that enables us to perform well. Indeed, we go from poor to good, from good to excellent and finally from excellent to outstanding. Certainly, as far as our core profession is concerned, then we should aim to be outstanding. To join, in other words, the 4 per cent[6] of truly outstanding performers, which is the 20 per cent of the 20 per cent according to the Pareto Principle. Coaching helps at every current level of performance, but for the seriously ambitious, who wish to become outstanding, there is a special fillip.

For it is certainly the case that most people want to work with, employ, contract, enjoy even, the top performers. We'd never deliberately choose to go to the worst doctor or dentist, would we? Similarly, if we care about results, we choose the best suppliers in all the fields of our work and our life. Put another way, coaching is especially relevant at the top end of performance because not only does it impact outcomes but it also becomes a form of marketing in itself. Jay Abraham,[7] the pre-eminent American marketing guru, often asserts that in marketing one of the key principles is to be perceived as 'pre-eminent', and to be pre-eminent in any field requires superior performance.

Performance has three elements to it (see Figure 2.4).

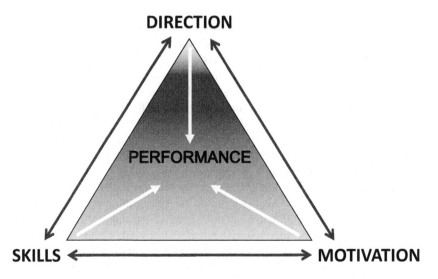

Figure 2.4 The performance triangle

All three elements are critical for success, but for the coach there has to be a starting point, and that usually is Direction. Before we know anything else, the client has to be clear about what they wish to achieve, where they are going (for example, where will they be in five years' time), and so all the skill in the world, and all the motivational energy, is going to be wasted if the client is going in the wrong direction. Therefore, a primary function of a great coach is to enable the client to establish with certainty that the direction they are heading is right for them (given that they have established rapport and motivation).

On top of this it is important that direction is aligned with motivators, otherwise the journey will go against the 'emotional grain' of the person; that will mean an increasing and corresponding difficulty as energy gets ever more depleted. In the final analysis, people who force themselves by willpower to do what they don't actually 'want' to do, become stressed and sick. For, as Paul Canon Harris[8] observed, "The main thing is to keep the main thing the main thing". The coach is there to help us find what that 'main thing' is, and it always involves a direction we have to go in to get it or to get there.

Before therefore we progress with this book we need to ensure that you feel like you have a clear direction – clarity, if you will, of what it is you want to create in your life.

At some level people have a deep feeling that their lives could be better; they know there is more available to them, and often they imagine future scenarios in which they see themselves happier and better than they are now. It's sometimes called 'day-dreaming': A picture, especially if the dream recurs, or a strong mental image starts forming in the mind. It begins to leave an imprint and we start strongly (as correspondingly strongly as the mental image forming) desiring this future or that end state. It may be that, say in five years' time, we see ourselves much wealthier or more successful in our career, or running a more fulfilling business, or in a new relationship or a much improved one, or that we are fitter, healthier in some way that makes us feel more attractive. We could go on, but these dreams to images to desires form the basis of what we might call a vision: A vision is seeing what may exist in the future now! And it is a homing mechanism; once you commit or lock onto a vision, *your* vision, you start the mobilisation of your own inner resources to meet the challenge. These inner resources are both your conscious intent and mental capacities, but also your subconscious mind, which must be aligned with your overt intent, otherwise self-sabotage occurs. We will return to the issue of congruence later, but let us consider vision in more detail.

It is important to bear in mind the 'double-bind' intrinsic to vision: First, a vision is a 'picture of the preferred picture'. Making the big picture real for oneself[9] is a distinctive competence and special responsibility.[10] This preferred picture has one basic premise: Things can be better than they are now.

The second 'bind' of a vision is a reason for being; thus, it is an 'emotional catalyst'. This is vital: Simply to point out where we are and gesticulate to where we want to be is a kind of 'gap analysis', but of a futile kind. Without an emotional catalyst the 'gap' might well be a cause for despair rather than effort. Furthermore, if we consider the notion of the 'preferred picture', then we can see that the importance of the word 'preferred' does not reside in our intellectual assent.

Oh, yes, it would be better if I had a successful business (but, sub-text, I'm not personally bothered). But in our emotional state, this preferred picture is something I really like and want – I want a successful business, this means something to me! In short, we identify with the preferred picture and it starts becoming part of our lives, our identities. This, in turn, generates what Charles Handy[11] calls the 'E-forces' of excitement, energy, enthusiasm, effort.

Thus, the coach is helping the client not only formulate a picture of the future, but is enabling the client to be 'emotionally catalysed' (or, to be less emotive, motivated) by the vision. The personal element is key; when a change agenda shifts from clichés, generalities and the obvious to an individual's hopes and dreams, and is expressed in their own words, it comes powerfully alive. What will kill a vision is insincerity; formulating a picture of a future that you don't really want and are not really committed to. If that sounds unlikely, and if you want to say, "But, who would do that?", the answer is, unfortunately, so many do. People decide, falsely as it were, against their own inner grain, that they should or ought to want this or to do that; oftentimes, these desires derive from childhood conditioning and the need for parental approval. They are powerful drives that need to be exposed to the light of self-awareness if they are ever to be surmounted.

One coaching technique that can help the client establish what is their real vision is by using the Motivational Map, for there will need to be an energetic alignment with the Map profile and the future vision.

ACTIVITY 2.3

Take a moment now to consider your vision for your future, say, five years from now (see Figure 2.5). How will it look? What will you be doing? What will you be experiencing? How will your life be playing out in the three major areas of your relationships, your career and your self-development or your personal growth? Jot down some notes. If you have not done a Map yet, go to note 12 of the Introduction to find out how to claim yours, and do one now. Compare your vision for the future with your top three motivators? Are they aligned? Are your motivators likely to support your quest to realise your vision? For instance, IF

> *Your vision is to be extremely rich BUT Builder is your lowest motivator ...*
> *Your vision is to be a senior level manager BUT Director is your lowest motivator ...*
> *Your vision is to be a creative designer BUT Creator is your lowest motivator ...*

Can you see that although the motivator sequence may not absolutely stop you realising your vision, their order is or can make a profound difference as to whether you are likely to achieve it simply because the lack of motivation in an

Motivator	Desirable central features of motivational vision	
DEFENDER	Will sustain long-term secure role?	Will have robust process and systems in place?
FRIEND	Will be part of a great team?	Will be socially engaged?
STAR	Will hold high profile position?	Will be in the spotlight?
DIRECTOR	Will lead and influence people?	Will manage resources?
BUILDER	Will prevail in competitive situations?	Will exploit commercial opportunities?
EXPERT	Will acquire deep learning?	Will deliver training commitments?
CREATOR	Will provide unique solutions?	Will generate creative applications?
SPIRIT	Will be boldly independent?	Will take my own decisions?
SEARCHER	Will make a difference?	Will fulfil my purpose?

Figure 2.5 Desirable central features of motivational vision

area that might naturally require it means that you do not really 'want' it in the same way as someone else for whom the motivator is dominant?

But once we have the vision we need to break the image down into manageable chunks – stepping stones, markers, do-able activities. As someone once joked, how do you eat an elephant? One bite at a time. The truth is a vision is too big a thing to achieve in one step or one move or one manoeuvre; it requires breaking down into specific goals, and these goals need addressing through specific actions. We will say more about choosing the right actions, the 20 per cent that make the real difference, in the next chapter.

The coach, then, must elicit from the client what their vision for the future is and consequently what goals follow from that (see Figure 2.6). And, the coach must also ensure there is an emotional – motivational – alignment between the vision and goals and the person's real feelings. This is a real challenge. But first, what is a goal?

ACTIVITY 2.4

Write down what your definition of a goal is; then check whether it covers the ground of our definition below.

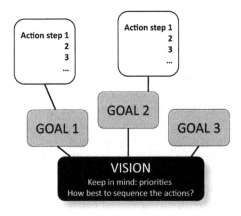

Figure 2.6 From vision to goals to action steps

A goal is essentially a desired result or anticipated outcome that a person imagines, plans and commits to achieve; it must have a deadline or time-frame or else it is simply a wish.

This last point is vital and takes us back to daydreaming, but not in a positive sense as before: many people find it easy to keep wishing that their life were other than it is; but without the urgency of time to drive them to action, the wishes remain wishes and never become true goals. In a strange way, whilst we can all bemoan the lack of time we experience, time properly understood is the spur that leads us to achieve. Time pressurises us to do more because it is limited; that said, of course, if we prioritise how we use our time, as per the 80/20 rule, there is plenty of time. As the great Roman, Seneca, put it: "Life is long enough, and it's given in sufficient measure to do many great things if we spend it well".

ACTIVITY 2.5

Consider the main areas of your life. These may be:

Work and Business
Health and Fitness
Personal Development, Growth, and Learning
Recreation and Play
Home and Family and Friends
Spirituality and Religion
Any other area of your life important to you? Write this down.

What is your timeframe for your goal? Do you work better with longer term or shorter term goals?

Now that you have the main areas of your life and a timescale to work towards, ask yourself what do you want to achieve in each area of your life in that timescale? Make a few bullet points and ensure you have considered each area of life (see Figure 2.7).

Now consider congruency. Keep in mind that we already have urged you to ensure that your vision and goals are congruent with your motivators. But there is a further congruence to consider. That is, does the domain or area of application of each goal complement the others, or are there elements of the goal which contradict or conflict with each other? For a truly effective goal we want all areas to work in harmony. This is not a compromise; it is instead actually considering what you really want in all of the areas of your life. Time is limited; if we consider relationships, achievement and growth and give them more familiar names such as family, career and personal development, respectively, it should be obvious that to get satisfaction in all three areas requires a delicate balancing act, and congruence. If, then, we spend all our time at and on work and our career, it will be difficult to sustain meaningful relationships or even to develop as a person. Equally, any other one category that is excessively focused on can have devastating consequences in the other areas. This principle applies at the main category level, but also at the smaller and more intimate goal setting level.

Thus, you need to consider congruency of your goals. Revisit the ones you have identified in Figure 2.7. Ask, are they congruent? The questions you have to ask

GOALS	MY GOALS	TIME SCALES	TOP 3 MOTIVATORS	CONGRUENT YES OR NO?
CAREER				
HEALTH				
LEARNING				
RECREATION				
FAMILY				
SPIRITUALITY				

Figure 2.7 Goals, motivators, and congruency

yourself if you are unsure are: can all these goals be achieved? Is there enough time in the next 3-6-9-12 months? Do I have enough resources to simultaneously work on all of these? And, if I had to prioritise, what would be the order of importance? Which have priority? Or put another way: Which is most important to you?

With these questions in mind, amend or refine any that are conflicting with each other but don't ditch them if they are important to you. Instead, change the level of expectation to one you feel you can meet, and yet stay aligned. A change of expectation might be: increasing the time frame for a promotion you want, reducing but not stopping one's other commitments, creating more boundaries around one's key relationships, especially perhaps with friends and so on.

Once you have refined the raw data of your goals, ensuring that they are congruent, a second need arises. Namely, the need to make the goal(s) as compelling to your subconscious mind as you possibly can. This is a critical point. Merely creating intellectual goals that the conscious mind assents to is not likely to succeed. There needs to be a deeper commitment from the whole you, your mind and your subconscious mind, to make goals work and be achievable. Your subconscious mind works through images, sounds and feelings; and it codes data, too, in that way. Every memory is coded symbolically with a unique set of pictures (and in an immeasurable number of combinations), sounds and feelings. This is how in a symbolic manner the subconscious mind stores everything that ever happens to us. It means of course that in some empirical sense our memories are not real; they are symbolic representations of our own reality. They are constructions the mind makes, albeit they seem very real to us. For many knowing this is a huge revelation, as they begin to understand that negative emotions from the past may not be the permanent fixture of their life they assumed they had to be. Fixtures which, of course, may well produce and play an over-bearing role in the outcomes of the future! Indeed, symbolic representations may well be de-constructed and others, better ones, substituted for them.

So how can we use this knowledge to our advantage with goal setting? Well, if you ever remember seeing a particular car which you like on the road for the first time, and you wanted it, you may have noticed that once you take specific note of *that* car, you begin to see it everywhere you go. What we focus on, in other words, grows in our experience.[12] Once something is in our conscious awareness we see opportunities. Is it that the cars and the opportunities were always there? Yes, but until we notice them we don't recognise them. Our minds can process 126 bits of information a second,[13] but within that same time frame we receive countless pieces of visual, auditory and kinaesthetic information bombarding our senses. What we pay attention to, therefore, has more to do with what is going on in our minds than in what we may term the external reality that is 'out there'. The mind, therefore, is more of a projector than a receiver; or, "perception is projection".[14]

With goal setting we can project our desired outcome by making it compelling to the subconscious mind by giving it a distinct visual, auditory and kinaesthetic quality.

ACTIVITY 2.6

To do this with your goals try the following activity.
   Write your goals and start with:

   I know I have achieved my goal when [put a specific date] ....

and go on to describe what you will see, hear and feel at this particular moment. The seeing, the hearing and the feeling are confirmation that the goal is actually achieved. So –

   What would you be seeing?
   What would you be hearing?
   What would you be feeling?
   Then go on to describe this event as if you were imagining the movie of it in your mind.

Thus, an example of a well written goal – imagine as a movie in your mind – might be this (see Figure 2.8):

BEVIS'S VISION

I know I have achieved my goal when on the 31st July 2017, I walk in the front door of my home and am immediately greeted by the smiling faces of my children. They are both super excited and jump into my arms as I walk inside the door. They have something they want to show me. As they take my hand and walk me through our home, they insist I close my eyes as they do and I can hear the excited murmurings of both, and the voice of Jules telling them to be careful. I am feeling fit, healthy, calm and energised after a Personal Training session that day, and I am enjoying my twice weekly workouts, weekly round of golf and daily meditations. They announce I can now open my eyes. I am not surprised but very pleased by what I see: the extension at the back of our home is now complete and I am looking out over an open plan kitchen dining area with a large wooden table capable of seating 10 comfortably with bench seating either side. The light comes in naturally through the Velux ceiling glass and through the windows to the front and side. Jules has done a fabulous job setting up the space with comfortable furnishings, making it a place to both eat and relax. The wood burner sits proudly to my right and I can feel the glow of heat emerging from it (not that we need it on today!) and the large rectangular cream floor tiles both add contrast to the kitchen and also neatly divide the two spaces. Aidan and Ellie rush me excitedly to the back doors and we open them and I can feel the fresh late afternoon summer's breeze on my face as we go out into the garden. Jules comes out with us and we decide to have a barbecue. Later, as we enjoy our family meal together, I reflect on the amazing six months we have had with our first book now written

Figure 2.8 Bevis Moynan thinking of his vision

in partnership with James Sale; our online business has gone from strength to strength with now over 100 online sign-ups; and financially we are stronger than ever, having recently doubled the amount we invest in our future each month.

Notice in the real example from Bevis that the vision of his future is power-fully envisaged in visual terms (the smiling faces, open my eyes, etc.), auditory terms (murmurings, voice, etc.) and kinaesthetic terms (jump into my arms, take my hand, etc.) In this way his future comes alive for him, becomes tan-gible, and the subconscious mind becomes excited by the images and feelings engendered by the activity. Essentially, what it then seeks is to have what it has in prospect as a reality; the subconscious, then, begins the process of 'attracting' reality to conform to the image, and it does this, naturally, subconsciously. It's not conscious work; it's an alignment of the subconscious mind with the inten-tions of the conscious one. Reality must be 'like' the image – this is the law of attraction.[15]

Dozens of books on what has been called 'the law of attraction' have been writ-ten, all extolling the virtue of such exercises; however, our intention, as much as understanding what it is that you want to achieve, is for you also to begin to realise at a deeper level what is really in the way of you achieving your goal!

In Chapters 5 and 6 we will explore the Limiting Beliefs and negative emo-tions which can often emerge the minute you set a new stretching goal. For the moment, however, if as you read your goal(s) any doubts or negative thoughts crop up just make a note of them (they will come in handy, too, for Chapters 4 and 7 especially).

Refining your goal: As you read your goal make sure that you check that it is:

a)   Stretching (most people when first writing a goal write something they can achieve comfortably). We tell our clients that we want them to fail repeatedly to achieve their 1-year goals; for as their life unfolds a much bigger can-vass emerges. Or, put another way, as you sail towards the horizon the view changes and one needs to adapt in the light of the new and more accurate perception of the way ahead. It is better to get 75 per cent of the way towards achieving a big goal – a big cake – than it is to set a much smaller goal and bake, successfully, a very small cake. This may seem to contradict the points we make on congruency; however, what we are looking for here is a balance between the goal being big and stretching and also congruent, so that no one element of the goal gets in the way of another.

b)   Pay attention to any lack of specificity; look out for any statements where you have used the classic vagueness of setting a goal like 'more money'. A good coach will respond, how much more specifically, and by when, and how will you know you have it? Be as specific as you can.

c)   Also note any areas of negation where you are really still thinking about what you don't want (this is far more common than you might think). For exam-ple: *I know I will have achieved my goal when I am no longer in this job that I hate and I stop feeling sluggish and miserable.* If your goal sounds like this, then what would be the opposite of what you have said be like? If you weren't feeling sluggish and miserable, how then would you actually be feeling? This is more important than we often can imagine, as we literally get in life what we focus on; therefore, at the outset we must make sure our subconscious thoughts are directed towards what we really want, as opposed to what we don't. Keep in mind, too, that to focus on what you don't want – on what you wish to avoid – is also to induce fear into your own subconscious, and fear usually paralyses rational action, creativity and effective decision-making. So, best to not go there!

The question of congruence, however, needs more and deeper exploration. For there are three major related but separate issues here. There is:

1 the congruence of the goals themselves
2 the congruence of each individual's motivators with their goals
3 the congruence of the goals and motivators with the individual's mission!

Mission and Vision are two quite different things. See Chapter 8 for more on mission. We need to remember that "Everything looks like failure in the middle. In nearly every change project doubt is cast on the original vision because problems are mounting and the end is nowhere in sight".[16] So, it is important not to give up too soon, to persevere. But that said, there are three major reasons why goal-setting fails, and to re-iterate: first, is *insincerity* – is the vision/goals what you really, really want? Second is *incongruence* – with other goals, other values, and with our own self-concept; and, finally, *imprecision* – a lack of clarity and of specifics, of being too vague and general. The coach, then, is one who challenges the client on clarity, alignment and desire; for when these three aspects converge, the client is truly empowered to go forward.

Summary

1 Coaching helps the client to become more self-aware, make the decision to change, and supports the client in both generating and completing actions to change and improve.
2 Self-awareness in the truest sense includes awareness of the body, mind, emotion and spirit.
3 Success for a client is success in all areas of life, with each area in harmony with the others.
4 Goals need to be aligned with the motivational preferences of the client.
5 Good goals cause clients to be emotionally driven by their contents.
6 Goals must have a timeline, a date by which they are achieved.
7 Congruency means that your goals include all areas of life important to you rather than focusing on just one at the detriment of others.
8 Goals need to be written, so that they evoke the senses, so that you see hear and feel them …
9 Goals need to be precise, sincere and congruent.

Notes

1 *A Complete Guide to the Soul*, Patrick Harpur, Rider, Ebury Publishing (2010).

2 *7 Habits of Highly Effective People*, Steven Covey, Simon and Schuster (1989).

3 *Man's Search for Meaning*, Viktor Frankl (1946).

4 *One Small Step Can Change your Life*, Dr Robert Maurer, Nightingale-Conant (2006).

5 *What's Right With the World*, GK Chesterton (1910).

6 20 per cent of people produce 80 per cent of the outcomes that are significant in any field, which is really a terrifying statistic, but one we find to be largely true. These clearly are the 'best' people in their profession. But the best of the best is the 20 per cent of the 20 per cent, which is 4 per cent of the total. These people truly are outstanding in terms of results, and so of course 'stand out'.

7 *Getting Everything You Can Out of All You've Got*, Jay Abraham, Judy Piatkus Publisher (2000), Chapter 4 - The Strategy of Pre-eminence.

8 *Leading for a Change*, Paul Canon Harris, Kevin Mayhew Publications (2016).

9 *Managing as a Performing Art,* Peter Vaill, Jossey-Bass (1989).

10 And especially of leaders who must also make it real to others; but keep in mind here that the call to personal development is the assumption of personal responsibility and one's own self-leadership in the process.

11 *Understanding Organisations*, Charles Handy, Penguin (1976/85).

12 *Flow*, Mihaly Csikszentmihalyi, Random Century Publishers (1992) - "Attention shapes the self, and is in turn shaped by it".

13 *Flow*: ibid. "The limitation of consciousness is demonstrated by the fact that to understand what another person is saying we must process 40 bits of information each second".

14 Originally this idea seems to derive from Jung: "We tend to take our most unconscious material and project it on people and events around us. That which is unconscious must of need be projected on people and events that are around us", and is cited by most NLP Practitioners, including Wayne Farrell, *Perception is Projection*, http://bit.ly/2tDbr6J.

15 According to Wikipedia, "the law of attraction is the belief that by focusing on positive or negative thoughts a person brings positive or negative experiences into their life". That - in a nutshell - is it. It seems simple; it is simple; but its implications are profound, and its practice, like acquiring any new habit, is not easy.

16 "Change is hardest in the middle", Rosabeth Moss Kanter, *Harvard Business Review* (August 2009), http://bit.ly/2tDbr6J.

3 Pareto, performance, and Motivational Maps

We are happy when we are in harmony; according to the Tao Te Ching,[1] in harmony with the Tao. The Tao is the Way – essentially, the natural flow of the universe and how it operates. It is an impersonal force according to the Tao Te Ching, but there is no problem in calling this 'God' if one wishes to. The point is that the universe conforms and complies with certain rules and principles and when we violate these we suffer. A simple and obvious example would be committing murder: all human societies have condemned the practice since the beginning of recorded time; and that murderers suffer is not only because if they get caught they are punished, but even if they are not caught history and literature provide ample testimony to the torments of the mind that they become prey to.[2] With this in mind, then, are there any natural laws of the universe that we inadvertently fail to respect or act upon? Laws whose existence we do not acknowledge or ignore, or whose tenets we flatly contradict or believe the opposite of?

There may be several[3] but there is certainly one which has huge ramifications on our everyday life, and on coaching practice in particular. One of the major issues affecting nearly everybody as a negative subconscious belief is that the universe works in a 50/50 way. Put another way, this means that all causes and inputs are more or less equal in terms of their symptoms and outputs. Again, a simple example illustrates the point: say, we get 100 (or 1000!) emails in our inbox and we wade through them as though they were all equally important, each one gets more or less the same amount of our time and attention. If that happens, then we are working on a 50/50 assumption about the nature of reality! We say IF it happens but in truth that is exactly what is happening all the time, since most of the time we are – unless we are incredibly disciplined – on some sort of automatic pilot or habitual mode of working whereby we deal with things as they turn up. In short, we may have heard of the Pareto Principle or 80/20 Rule as it is sometimes called, but very few people (surely less than 20 per cent?) do anything about it (see Figure 3.1). Some emails are much more important than others, and often that 'some' is about 20 per cent of the total. So, the universe works in an asymmetrical or 80/20 way, not a 50/50, all-things-equal way. Things are not equally important. If we wish to be effective, we have to identify the 20 per cent of activities that cause or

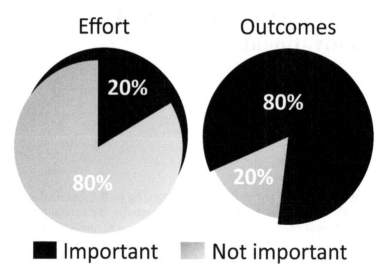

Figure 3.1 Pareto 80/20 effort v. outcomes

create 80 per cent of our overall results; and if we go further and '80/20' the 80/20 we realise that 4 per cent of inputs will generate 64 per cent[4] of outputs. If we are going to coach effectively this is an astonishing statistic to get our head round for the client.

But from a performance, and so from a coaching perspective, this principle, like Motivational Maps, is a key pillar of effective coaching. Because we cannot do everything, there is an ongoing necessity to prioritise, and this prioritisation requires that we think; and particularly that, as Richard Koch[5] puts it, we "think 80/20".

Let us be clear about this now: 80/20 is not an exact figure. The percentage of inputs may vary, and indeed it is a primary purpose of coaches to skew this ratio. (And they do this by the intervention of coaching.) Though the starting point might be not 80/20 but 70/30 or 60/40 or 90/10 or 95/5, whatever it is, it is not 50/50. It also needs to be said that whilst the Pareto Principle holds true in most life and business situations, there can be exceptions. It is generally true, for example, that for most businesses 20 per cent of the customers generate 80 per cent of the revenues; but that *probably* doesn't work in, say, the supermarket model[6] where 20 per cent of customers probably do not account for 80 per cent of revenues. But as far as coaching, consultancy, training and other service industries are concerned, it is uncannily accurate, as it will be for most sectors and most non-commodity businesses.

With this in mind then, let us return to performance. We saw in Chapter 2 that performance has three elements to it: Direction, Skills (an umbrella term which includes knowledge too), and Motivation. When coaching clients, coaches can focus on all these three elements equally. Clearly, however, for themselves and their business, the most important element is Direction (as discussed in

Chapter 2) as this will help to develop a relevant business model. But working within organisations – and career coaching aside (see Chapter 7) – often the performance issue is only really down to two elements: Skills and Motivation. Why is this? Because the Direction is often set by the organisation, and embedded in detailed business and strategic plans whereby there is not a lot of room for individual manoeuvre or even input. Clearly, the more junior you are, the less influence you generally have anyway on direction. But even at senior level, one might simply be committed to following the plans the Board or Senior team has formulated. Thus, performance comes down to two elements: Skills and Motivation.

We can express this in a simple formula (see Figure 3.2)[7]:

Performance = Skills × Motivation, or P = S × M[8]

ACTIVITY 3.1

If you score yourself out of 10 as a coach – or in any role you currently are in – for your overall sense of how skilful you are (not forgetting that Skill here includes knowledge too), then do the same out of 10 for how motivated you are. Multiply these two figures; these will give you a Performance number; and this is actually a Performance percentage or Rating, since the maximum is out of 100.

My Performance Rating (PR) is: ?? per cent ... What does this mean to me?

The Pareto Principle can help us to understand what this means. But, before we get to that, there is one other interesting aspect of this: we can rate ourselves and self-rating can be very accurate, but in order to get an even stronger grip on how we are performing, how do other people rate us (see Figure 3.3)?

Figure 3.2 Performance is: Skills *times* Motivation

	Skills/10	Motivation/10	Performance %
You			
Associate			
Client			
Others			
Average scores			

Figure 3.3 Performance assessment table

ACTIVITY 3.2

Ask others to score you in the same way as you have done yourself. Obviously, you will only select people who are positively disposed towards you for this exercise. If you are a coach, the useful people to ask would be associates who may work with you on projects or clients, as well as clients themselves. 'Others' could include subordinates at work, peers or even your boss.

Of course, it's all very well scoring yourself on your generic motivation rating; there is also an easy way to check this – by doing a Motivational Map and converting the PMA percentage score into a number out of 10, simply by rounding it up and down: so 74 per cent would be 7/10 and 75 per cent would be 8/10 and so on. But is the Skill rating not more complex? For, though it is true that we can consider the overall impact of our skills (and knowledge), at some point we recognise that we need to isolate more exactly what these skills are and then carry out another rating for each one individually.

ACTIVITY 3.3

Make a list of your top 10 skills and knowledge areas.[9] Rank order them. Which are the most important in terms of work success and performance? And if you have 10 skills (or areas of knowledge), then 2 or 3 according to the Pareto Principle will be responsible for the majority of your success. Identify these 2 or 3 key skills. When you have done this you might ask: how can I leverage these even more? Jot down any ideas you have.(Use the table in Figure 3.4.)

Key Skills	Component Skills	8+ Zone	6+ Boost	3+ Risk	3- Action	Comments Actions
Building Rapport	empathic					
	listening					
	motivating					
Questioning	listening					
Goal Setting	challenging					
	focused					
	intuitive					
↑			**Pareto 20% ?**			
Consistent Approach	organised					
Holding to Account						
Curiosity						
Expert Toolkit & Ideas	NLP					
Objectivity	Realistic					
Process Orientated						
Flexible						
↑			**Pareto 80% ?**			

Figure 3.4 Coaching skills table

What are, then, the key skills of coaching?

Note: if the Pareto Principle is true, which it almost certainly is here,[10] then of these 10 key coaching skills, 2 or 3 (that is to say 20 or 30 per cent of them will be mission critical and more important than the others).

ACTIVITY 3.4

Compare your top 10 list with ours; keep in mind we are not saying your list is invalid, but are there any learning points from our list for you? Review again your list of top 10 coaching skills and, if you think appropriate, incorporate any ideas or suggestions that you think fit from ours. Three key learning points here are:

1   What are the 2 or 3 skills you simply have to be great at in order to be an effective coach?
2   What skill have you scored lowest? Consider what the implications of that are for your clients. Is there any action you need to take?
3   Now consider the skill you have rated highest —if you have not totally mastered it, what do you have to do to get there?

Keep in mind that although there may be some skills/knowledge that all coaches[11] will need to have, it could also be the case that you as a coach work in a niche area in which some seemingly unimportant skill or knowledge area becomes of critical importance. For example, personal coaches who work in the sports arena may well need as a core component either knowledge of health and physiology, or even of a specific activity or game to function at the highest level. Or both!

But we return now, then, to the question of what does this all mean and how can it help us coach effectively? The first important thing to grasp about the Pareto Principle is in the numbers: 80/20. This is a 4:1 ratio and it suggests two important things that everyday experience bears out.

One, that it means the top 20 per cent of the workforce will produce 80 per cent of the results; conversely, two, the other 80 per cent of the workforce will produce only 20 per cent of the results. You need to reflect on the enormous and (for most businesses) unwelcome implications of this.

The maths goes like this:

If 20% of Employee-A (E_A) produces 80% of total Results (R), and
If 80% of Employee-B (E_B) produces 20% of total Results (R), then
$20E_A = 80R_A$ so $E_A = 80/20R_A = 4/1 = 4 \times R_A$ (four times the average result, R_A)

and

$80E_B = 20R_A$ so $E_B = 20/80R_A = 1/4 = 0.25 \times R_A$ (one quarter the average result, R_A).

So

$E_A/E_B = 4/0.25 = 16/1 = 16$ times!

In other words, some employees (and for that matter coaches and managers) are up to 16 times more productive than others. Since we know that productivity is a function of performance,[12] then we know also that Skills and Motivation are core to being productive. Being productive, of course, is the central benefit that organisations want from their employees; and employees want that benefit for themselves because it boosts their own self-esteem as well as their career and earning prospects. Furthermore, this ratio of 4/1 and 16 times gives a clue as to how to frame this information: if at the extremes someone is 16 times more productive than another person, what 'rating' is the average person going to be? The answer is clearly 1: the average person is going to be 1 times more productive than the average person! Which is 1. So, 1 is the midpoint between the performance extremes of 4 and ¼ ($4 \times ¼ = 1$; $4 \div 4 = 1$). So truly productive people are 4 times more productive than the average person, and up to 16 times more productive than the least productive person; keep in mind that this number holds more constant the larger the number of people we are dealing with, and we have already said that 80/20 may skew to be more – 70/30 – or less that way – 90/10. But with that in mind, we now have a scale on which to rate performance as a function of skill and motivation.

Skills/Knowledge and Motivation are for rating purposes either at below average, average, above average, or optimum (see Figure 3.5):

This language may seem dry and academic: average and optimum. Some people find it easier to correlate the numbers with more emotive language. It is not important which words you choose especially, so long as one is consistent. Figure 3.6 shows our favourite interpretation of the four rating numbers:

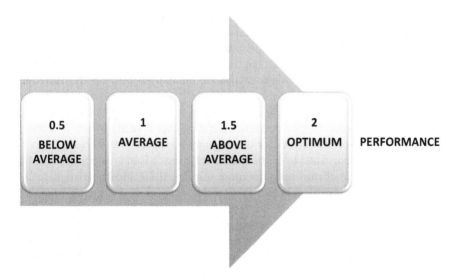

Figure 3.5 Skills and Motivation four-point scale – generic language

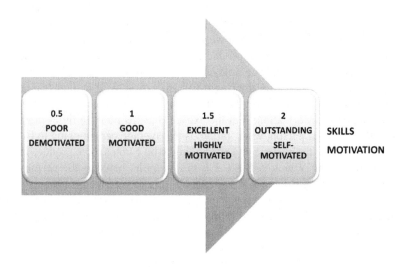

Figure 3.6 Skills and Motivation four-point scale – specific language

Note that 'average' has now become a 'good' (for skills), a much more emotive and positive word. People prefer to be good than average; but we need to be clear about what we are saying here. Actually 'good' is often average. We say, 'good job', or 'you're doing a good job', and usually what that means is: you are simply doing the job as it needs to be done. The problem with it is: doing a good job, at organisational level, is never 'good' enough. It always withholds that extra discretionary effort that is at the heart of what is called engagement. It also leads employees to become very frustrated and disappointed by their employers: they are told that they are 'good', but there seems to be no extra remuneration or reward for being good – which is to say, simply doing your job properly. And from the employers' perspective, why would there be? 'We' pay you to do the job; you do it – that's the deal. Why does that entail extra rewards? That's their reasoning. Hence 'good' is good but we need to understand that it really means average.[13] And it is the job of the coach – or the manager internally – to increase the performance of the individual by shifting the Performance Rating score upwards by either enabling the client to acquire more relevant skills and knowledge, or by increasing their motivation, which leads to an increase of energy. Or by doing both simultaneously.[14]

However, there is a missing number here, which is 0. Zero, however, is not a number; it is an absence – no performance at all. So what we are saying in the scale of performance – and actually of motivation and skills too – is that there are four levels AND +1, where '+1' is no performance at all. And no performance at all can result either from a complete lack of motivation or a complete lack of the necessary skills and knowledge in and for a specific role. We have all doubtless seen just such an eventuality in action many times before: but people who cannot perform at all are usually quickly shown the door, or run businesses that fail almost immediately.

If we now then plot Skills/Knowledge against Motivation, we can create a Performance Rating Index (see Figure 3.7).

For the coach, what we want to do is to help the client generate a Performance Rating (PR) of '4'; in other words, to be totally on top of their game: fully motivated and wholly equipped with all the right skills and knowledge to do their job or perform their role effectively. Therefore, the question becomes what is the issue – Skills or Motivation – that is holding the client back? Where do they sit on the Rating Index? Indeed, where do you, in your current position, sit on the Rating Index?

ACTIVITY 3.5

Imagine you are a coach working at the ABC company and they have asked you to run a 6-month coaching programme to improve the performance of five team members: Jon, Chris, Sue, Petra, and Sam. You as the coach ask their manager to position each one of them on the Motivation–Skills grid. And you ask the manager to do this not by the numbers, but by the emotive language we used earlier. First skills: Are they, skill-wise:

> *poor   good   excellent   outstanding?*

You translate the manager's answers to a number on the grid. Then you do the same for their respective motivations. Are they, motivation-wise:

> *demotivated   motivated   highly   motivated   self-motivated?*

You do the same for these words and convert them to one of the four numbers on the grid. At this point you have the five clients distributed as on the grid, Figure 3.8. What, then, is the issue of each of these five individuals based on their position on the grid? Make some notes and then compare them with our suggestions.[15]

One, of course, can ask a manager for their view of their employees from a skills or motivational view point at the first meeting. Ideally, however, you will want the employees (and the manager) to have completed a Motivational Map. This will reduce even further the guesswork as to which motivational quadrant the client is actually in; and it will certainly be more accurate. For managers often do not see

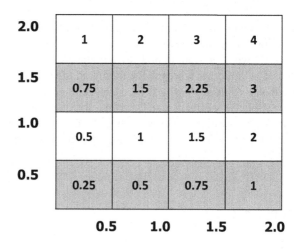

Figure 3.7 Performance Rating (PR) Index

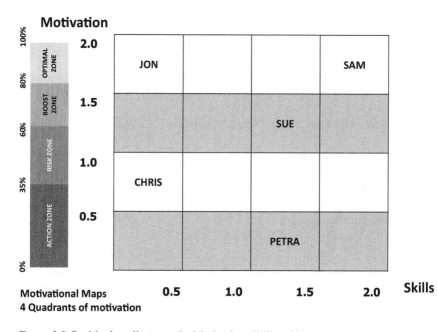

Figure 3.8 Positioning clients on the Motivation–Skills grid

either what is really motivating an employee or how motivated they are; seeing whether they have the skills or knowledge to do the job is much more visible and evident. But with motivation people, not just at work, put on a front or face and show what they think their boss (or their partner or their friends) wants to see. We have regularly in our own practice as coaches come across managers and bosses who have been shocked by the actual level of motivation revealed by the Map: they thought, for example, their 'star' member of the sales team loved their work, and certainly had been pulling in the results, but the Map had revealed that they were running on empty. Yes, they had the skills to do the job effectively, but increasingly their heart wasn't in it; they were faking it to try and make it, and invariably had some exit plan they were going to implement in some short order soon!

If we look at Figure 3.8 again, we see imposed alongside the Y axis of motivation the four quadrant image that appears in all Motivational Maps on page 13 of the report. And just as we have said that 80/20 is not exact, but a varying approximation, so here with the four quadrants, we need approximations to reality to describe what is going on. But in essence the four quadrants, descriptively, become zones of motivational energy. The top level, which is 80%+, is called the Optimal Zone. The challenge of being in the Optimal Zone is to stay there; there are so many drains on our energy. How do we minimise them and stimulate the activities and events that genuinely boost our energy? The second level, from 61–80% motivated, we call the Boost Zone. This is a high level of motivation at the top end, but clearly trailing off as we approach the 61% mark. It is called Boost because we do need to boost this person's motivation to get them into the Optimal Zone, or simply to get them higher within the Boost Zone itself.

60 per cent is the actual crunch point. We are in the third zone, the Risk Zone (35–60%). Seemingly, 60 per cent is quite a high score – a good score – but as with 'good' before, it is average and people at this level have certainly lost their 'mojo' for work and what they do. One or two of their top motivators are no longer being fulfilled in a meaningful way; they are in fact at risk of becoming demotivated. To be kind we could call this a 'good' level of motivation, but, in reality, it is a falling away of the essential, brim-full levels of energy we really need to achieve anything great.

In zone 4, the Action Zone (10–34%),[16] we truly are not motivated at all. In truth, this is a state of motivational torpor and it is very dangerous for our health if we stay in it for a long time. That is, if we are in a job/role that totally does not motivate us, fails to ignite our emotional fires, goes contrary to how we feel and what we want from life, and so on, then the inevitable will happen: We become stressed and our well-being suffers. And, although people have differing levels of inner resistance and resilience, prolonged exposure to this sort of situation will lead to breakdown or illness of some sort. So this is called the Action Zone because it is imperative for the client and for the coach to understand radical action is necessary to change this situation; and this radical action has to include the possibility of quitting the role as well as any other major shift or focus.

With this in mind, then, if we now look at Figure 3.9 we see how the Motivational score from the Map can be translated into a Pareto score for the purposes of using the $P = S \times M$ formula.

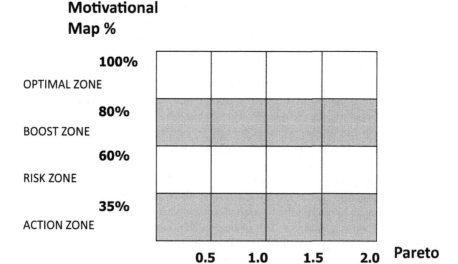

Figure 3.9 Converting Motivational Map scores to Pareto rating scores

ACTIVITY 3.6

Consider the following scores from a Motivational Map. Decide which Pareto score would you assign each one of these to. For example, if someone scored 85 per cent in their Map then that would be a Pareto score of 2.

Map score: Pareto score[17]
37%
64%
34%
59%

One central purpose of coaching and of the tool, Motivational Maps, is to skew the Pareto Principle. As we said before, it is almost impossible to get the Pareto ratio to be 50/50 – only a tiny company *could* do that and probably only for a short time: it would mean everybody is equally productive! The larger the company, the more they revert to the 80/20 mean. But we can – through interventions like Motivational Maps and its reward strategies, coaching and training – skew the 80/20 to 70/30 or even 60/40: this has a huge impact on productivity and the bottom-line.

Take the typical ratio of 80/20. If instead of 20 per cent producing 80 per cent, we had 40 per cent producing 80 per cent and 60 per cent producing 20 per cent we will have double the number of people being productive – in short the 100 per cent is going to be a much bigger cake!

To get, then, a sense of how important this is, and what it might mean for the bottom-line of an organisation, whether commercial or not-for-profit, we need to consider this. The PR – the Performance Rating – has implications for the finances of any company. If you recall our discussion regarding the PR of 1, the average, then it stands to reason that the average organisation pays the average employee an average salary or wage that is, pretty much exactly, what that person is worth to the organisation. In short, the average person is paid to be productive and to produce more in productivity than what they are paid. If they are not more productive than their salary, then the organisation will quickly become bankrupt because they will be paying more in salaries than they are achieving in productivity gains.

With that in mind, let's consider the client who is an employee. Tony works for XYZ. The total costs of employing Tony are, say, £40,000 per year. Total costs mean salary plus National Insurance, pension contributions etc. – everything it costs the organisation to hold onto Tony.

If Tony were an average – good – employee his PR would be 1. He would be doing his job and adding some value. We could frame his position like this as in Figure 3.10:

But suppose that we coach Tony and his motivation or his skills improve as a result. What then? His skills improve or his motivation increases, so his new PR is 1.5. What then?

Tony   £40,000 1.5   £40,000 × 1.5 = £60,000

So now we can add more details (see Figure 3.11):

Client	Total Cost	Performance Rating	Resource Valuation (RV)
Tony	£40,000	1	£40,000 x PR of 1=£40,000

Figure 3.10 Map client Resource Valuation

Client	Total Cost	Current PR	Resource Valuation	Post Coaching PR	Future RV	Increase RV
Tony	£40K	1	£40K	1.5	£60K	£20K

Figure 3.11 Map client Resource Valuation (RV) increase

If we consider Figure 3.7 again we can see that the possible multiples include: 0.25. 0.5, 0.75 which would all mean someone performing below the average and thus making a loss for the organisation; to 1, which is average; to 1.5, 2, 2.25, 3 and 4, which all mean substantial productivity gains.

The calculation also gives us a way of seeing clearly who is productive and by how much; and also following the coaching intervention, who can grow and improve, and who cannot. This is priceless information. It may be objected that this is subjective, since the PR is subjective. But is that really true? We base the motivational score component on the actual Motivational Map where we have a perceived Face Validity accuracy score of 95 per cent; that's pretty accurate. And as for the Skills assessment number, how likely is that to be wrong, since from the dawn of management, managers have been accurately reckoning the relative strengths of their employees' skills and knowledge and spending billions of pounds a year to get staff up to speed? All in all, then, carried out without prejudice, this is likely to be a highly accurate picture of the performance profile of the client.

There is one final aspect of this $P = S \times M$ formula that is worth commenting on. That is, the curious and unexpected effect of the multiplication of the numbers. If, for example, we think the client's motivation is 60 per cent or 6/10 – the Risk Zone – and their skill score is 6/10 or 60 per cent, average or good too – then the actual performance is not 6/10 or 60 per cent. It is 6×6 or 36 per cent! And if we put this in Pareto terms, this becomes 1×1, which is JUST in the third zone, so is still 1, but it is at the bottom end of it. The 10 scale gives us here a finer tuning; but the drift is clear – the multiplying factor dilutes performance, and so it is critical, first, for the coach to understand that if they wish to get their client into the Optimal Zone of performance, the lowest scores that make that possible are 9 and 9.

Skills 9/10 × Motivation 9/10 = 81% performance or being in the Optimal Zone.

ACTIVITY 3.7

Coaches themselves, then, need to be at 9 and 9 – to be in the zone of motivation and of skills! If you did Activities 3.2 and 3.3, then you will have scored yourself and even got feedback from others scoring you. The question for the coach now – and for anyone else who needs to perform – is how do we get to 9/10 in terms of our motivational level and our skill set?

Look at the grid in Figure 3.12 and ask yourself how you can improve your scores in the three top motivational areas and the three core skills that you have identified as being critical to your business.

Your top three motivators will be established from your Map profile, along with a score out of 10 for each one of them separately on page 13 of the report. If you have scored 10/10 for any one or all of them, then you clearly cannot improve on

Motivator	Current Score/10	Goal to improve score	Time frame	Actions
1				
2				
3				
Skill				
1				
2				
3				

Figure 3.12 Performance Action Plan

that, but you might ask yourself how you can maintain it – keep in mind that motivation is like health or fitness: it has to be continually worked on. And regarding your skill set, which you addressed in Figures 3.3 and 3.4, then be clear about what being 10/10 in terms of skill/knowledge really means: ask, am I comparing myself against others, a normative assessment, or against some fixed standards, criteria referenced? Even if at 10/10, think 80/20: the next iteration of the 80/20 on the top 4 per cent of performers. That would mean being not in the top 4 per cent but the top 0.8 per cent! The Pareto Principle suggests that the top 0.8 per cent reap over 50 per cent of the rewards[18] – so a dedicated commitment to becoming even better than the best one can be has tremendous implications for future rewards.

Finally, and briefly in this chapter, it would be inappropriate not to mention a cousin of the Pareto Principle, namely, Kaizen,[19] since it has profound coaching implications. Kaizen is a process of continuous improvement in which over a long period of time one seeks to make small, incremental improvements to processes or systems in order to improve their efficiency or quality. The Japanese spectacularly used this idea, especially in their automotive and electronics industries, to become world leaders in their fields. It should be clear why this is a cousin of the Pareto Principle: It's finding what appear to be small, sometimes inconsequential items, and improving them that can lead to massive gains. In short, the 20 per cent – or even 1 per cent of inputs – that can make the big difference to the outcomes.

So far as coaching goes this is important because one aim of the coach is to get the client to adopt new habits or rituals that are more helpful to them than the ones that led them to their issue. We talk about the client taking action – see Figure 3.12 for a standard case of 'actions' that follow the coaching process; but how do these positive actions become habits or rituals (like cleaning our teeth every morning) that we do without thinking? The trouble is, we know from our own experience that we commit to doing something – like dieting, exercising, studying the financial accounts, making the sales calls, confronting the difficult employee, etc. – and we do it once, but then we fall away from making it our consistent practice. Usually, this is because the 'ask' is too much and we despair of keeping going. Forming new habits or rituals, then, is a key element of successful coaching.

Here's where Kaizen helps, for it can enable us to shape small, micro-habits that produce awareness, micro-practice, repetition, progress and a deeper level of embedding the required behaviour. In his One Small Step programme, Dr Robert Maurer[20] provides from Kaizen perhaps the most brilliant question of all that a coach (and self-coach) can ask themselves which propels one forward:

Key Kaizen Question:

What is the smallest possible step I could take towards my destination?

And then one does that step for as long as is comfortable. Then, increase the step – do more – and build up. Suppose fitness were an issue. We don't start by committing to a marathon run, or swimming a mile front crawl. We start with something really small – like walking to the local shop where before we used to take the car; or doing one length, or width even, in a pool (based on where we are now) – and persist at doing that. This has a remarkable effect on our resolution and stick-ability. Over time we find so much is possible in terms of new habits, patterns of behaviour, and our ability to change positively.

ACTIVITY 3.8

Ask yourself, what is your current most important goal; and what is the smallest possible step you could take towards achieving it? Take that step! Start forming that habit. Continually build on this process and ask yourself daily or weekly this same question.

Summary

1 We are happy when we are in harmony with the natural flow of the universe.
2 The Pareto Principle states that 20 per cent of actions (approximately) will deliver 80 per cent of your results.
3 Performance is a combination of Direction, Skills, and Motivation.
4 For many working within an organisation, where direction is clearly set from above, this can be simplified to Performance = Skills × Motivation.

5   Some employees are up to 16 times more productive than their colleagues.

6   Using a Skills and Motivation four-point scale allows focus on where improvements really need to be made for each individual and gives an indication of its potential impact.

7   For true performance we need both highly motivated and highly skilled individuals.

8   Kaizen is a process of continuous improvement in which over a long period of time one seeks to make small, incremental advances.

9   Forming new habits is a key outcome of successful coaching; and facilitating a client's awareness of the smallest possible step aids this process whilst minimising potential fatigue or concern of failure.

Notes

1   *Tao Te Ching* - Lao Tzu, Richard Wilhelm Edition, Penguin (1985).

2   "O, full of scorpions is my mind, dear wife!"- Macbeth, William Shakespeare.

3   For an overview take a look at Richard Koch's *The 80/20 Principle and 92 Other Powerful Laws of Nature*, Nicholas Brealey (2014); a worthy sequel to his original book on Pareto and which explains '92' other laws that operate in life.

4   *80/20 Sales and Marketing*, Perry Marshall, Entrepreneur Press (2013).

5   *The 80/20 Principle*, Richard Koch, Nicholas Brealey Publishing (1997).

6   *Pareto's Principle,* Antoine Delers, Lemaitre Publishing (2015).

7   One source for this model, although it does not incorporate using Motivational Maps, is Gill Sanderson's article, 'Objectives and Evaluation', to be found in *The Handbook of Training and Development,* edited by Steve Truelove, Blackwell (1995).

8   For a more advanced formula than this see our book, James Sale and Steve Jones, *Mapping Motivation for Engagement*, Routledge, due out in late 2018, where other key factors in the performance mix are addressed, especially the concept of 'commitment', which is allied to motivation but not the same as. One needs to reiterate again that the models are approximations to reality, and not reality itself; just as the 80/20 itself is not exactly always 80/20 - indeed is usually not 80/20 but working on its approximations can give us so much insight.

9   If you go on-line, you will find very little agreement between experts on what the ten most important skills are. For example, Forbes' list - http://bit.ly/2p9Bktx - is very different from the top 10 of the International Institute of Directors and Managers: http://bit.ly/2ouYdGT.

10 These skills are of course all technical skills; for the sake of clarity we have omitted the marketing, sales and other business skills that a coach will necessarily have to master in order to be effective. Also, note too that not all the skills are actually skills: listening is a skill, as is questioning, but being consistent is perhaps more a quality.

11 Again, we are here referring to technical, coaching skills; of course, a self-employed coach will also need to do the same activity to cover business, marketing, finance and sales skills that are necessary to run a business.

12 To perform at a high level and not to be productive would almost certainly be a question of either misdirection or being misdirected; in other words, that the individual has inappropriate or unsuitable goals, plans and strategies surrounding their work. The third element of the performance triangle, then, would need to be addressed either by the individual or by their manager - and both can be addressed through coaching.

13 And without wishing to confuse everyone, 'average' can mean, in a top performing organisation, 'mediocre'. So we have the paradox that when somebody might say,

'That is a good performance', then they mean it is mediocre! The reverse is also true: an over-demanding, perfectionistic boss might well describe an employee's performance as 'mediocre' when in fact it is 'good' - which is to say, average; they are doing the job.

14 And, of course, preceding both skills and motivation, especially if we are discussing career coaching, then helping the client find their vision, set appropriate goals and targets - to go in the right direction - is also critical.

15 The main issue for Chris is skill, though motivation is only good (average); and skill is a big issue for Jon. Given how motivated Jon is, it may be he is new (hence hasn't acquired the skills yet) and needs induction. Petra is skilled but not motivated - could be that she has been there a long time. Sue has equal motivation and skill PR scores, so here the coach needs to probe sensitively to discover where the maximum leverage might be. And for Sam - PR 4 - in the zone of performance, the issue is one of sustaining that: how do we keep motivation and skill set up and finely honed over the next 12 months? In such a situation, usually, keeping motivation high is the priority, and the skills will follow.

16 The lowest possible motivational score is 10 per cent in Motivational Maps.

17 37% is in the Risk Zone; 64% is Boost Z; 34% is Action Z; and 59% is Risk Z.

18 52% in fact: Perry Marshall. Ibid.

19 *Kaizen: The Key to Japan's Competitive Success*, Masaaki Imai, McGraw-Hill (1986/91).

20 *One Small Step Can Change your Life*, Dr Robert Maurer, Nightingale-Conant (2006).

4   Coaching, NLP, and Motivational Maps

So far we have covered several angles on coaching, motivation and performance; now we would like to explore links between coaching, NLP, and Motivational Maps. NLP stands for Neuro Linguistic Programming, which was developed in the 1970s by Richard Bandler and John Grinder.[1] By studying several world class therapists and modelling – imitating – their processes for success with patients, they came up with a series of 'pillars' and principles that underpin their methodology. The 'Four Pillars of NLP'[2] are:

1   *Setting your goals – clarifying what you want*
2   *Using your senses – paying close attention to everything for clues and cues*
3   *Behaving flexibly – not getting stuck in patterns, routines that don't work*
4   *Building relationships – recognising the necessity of others' support to achieve goals*

These pillars are entirely compatible with what we have said so far. One constant and recurring theme has been the 'invisible': *there* in the subconscious, those imperceptible threads it seems to weave, and how we experience problems we can't quite put our finger on. These keep us stuck until we can bring them into conscious awareness, and clearly Motivational Maps and coaching are two powerful mechanisms for doing this.

Bringing problematic subconscious thoughts and patterns to the surface is literally like shining a flashlight on a dark corner of a room: all of a sudden you can see clearly. From an NLP perspective gaining that insight means we are at least 50 per cent or more forward in solving the problem. Let's review what we have established as core coaching skills in Chapter 3. In Figure 4.1 are the top three skills that coaches need to deploy.

NLP as a modality has a whole section dedicated to building rapport and also teaches linguistic skills that contribute to the ability to question, listen and to assist clients in gaining clarity of direction through goal setting. NLP also, however, requires two other important commitments to the coaching process:

4:    That the client is 100 per cent responsible[3] for that outcome; they take responsibility
5:    Stillness, or presence (from and of the coach)

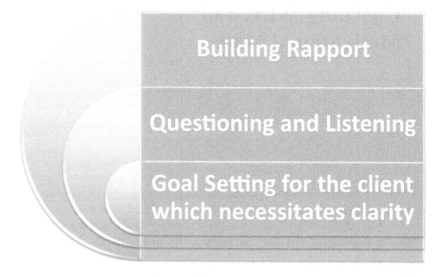

Figure 4.1 Top three coaching skills

Clearly, points 4 and 5 are not exactly skill sets, but effective coaching depends on them. The importance of taking responsibility is a double whammy: on the one hand, by taking responsibility the client grows or matures as a person, which means it's developmental; and, secondly, it prevents any 'game' playing that might subvert the coaching process. Not just in coaching, but in advising anyone generally, we probably have all experienced that seemingly 'hungry' person who wants our advice and then subsequently and inexplicably does the opposite of what they say they will do or does nothing at all. This game playing is the antithesis of effective coaching, and so the client taking responsibility up front is vital. It also means that denial, projection and blame are all 'no-no's in the coaching intervention. The NLP coach then is asking in a gentle manner for complete commitment to the process; after all there is a realisation that it is the client who makes the changes and the NLP coach is merely the facilitator of that change.

Point 5, however, is just as important, yet seemingly not much at all: stillness or presence. It is, perhaps, here that NLP coaching differs most from traditional coaching in that we are working with both the conscious and subconscious minds of our clients. Traditional coaching can get by with, say, a GROW model that simply reviews Goals, Reality, Options and Wrap-Up, but doesn't necessarily (although a great coach using the model will) go into the subconscious and its own strange and emotional logic.[4] So NLP deliberately steps into and wants to investigate the subconscious blocks to performance and help the client to overcome those types of blocks.

What, then, is stillness, or presence and how does it help? Stillness is that process by which we become entirely present and in the moment.[5] We refrain from thinking about the future or the past; and we do this through some meditative practices, all of which have at their root, control of breath and breathing techniques.

But, you may well be asking, how does this help the client? You are 'present', engaged in some meditation[6] technique, how is that helpful?

It helps the client in at least three profound ways: first, it extends and deepens the quality of the listening that the coach is able to supply. We said before that listening is an act of love; when the coach is able to centre their self and be entirely present, then listening is qualitatively and quantitatively enhanced. Second, this kind of still-ness excludes judgement, which always creates barriers for the client. And third, the coach by stilling their own mind is able to access a profounder level of understanding and response, including the formulation of better questions. We call this in NLP 'intuitive questioning', because the questions are not logically worked out and pre-formulated but arise from the very encounter itself. NLP teaches the linguistic skills of being very specific,[7] yet the ability to be hypnotically vague; and this provides a framework for questioning in the form of a detailed personal history. Here, perhaps, we may note the difference between a relatively new NLP coach who is following a format, and an experienced NLP coach who is practising asking questions intuitively, trusting in their subconscious mind or, to put it another way, trusting presence.

Unsurprisingly, then, intuitive questioning cannot be taught. In a way the role of the NLP coach mirrors the client process: both coach and client are accessing their subconscious in order to find solutions.

Deep wisdom traditions believe that in these moments we are actually tapping into something beyond even our subconscious mind; that we are tapping into the "Collective Unconscious"[8] or "Universal Mind". Theologically speaking, this would be equivalent to hearing the voice of God or a god (as the Greeks did in their cult centres). Whatever the terminology or metaphor used, the key point to grasp is that the universal testimony of mankind is that there is a wisdom inherent in altered mind states[9]; for this is essentially what happens when we start to be still and control our breathing.

Quietening the mind, then, is to prepare for a coaching session.

ACTIVITY 4.1

Sit comfortably, both feet flat on the floor, and close your eyes and place your attention on your breathing; breathe in through the nose and gently, naturally out through the mouth. Do a slow count up to 27 on the outbreath if that helps, and repeat this if you need to. After you begin to feel yourself relax, see if you notice the energy in your body, perhaps a light tingling sensation in the hands or the feet, or an awareness of energy in the arms or chest or stomach.

Stay present in this exercise until you notice the energy within the body, and then aim to have a conversation with someone whilst maintaining that awareness of your inner body and notice what happens.

Write down your experiences and reflections here:

_____
_____
_____

ACTIVITY 4.2

Hakalua[10] Stillness Exercise

Again sit comfortably with your feet flat on the floor and find a spot above eye level that you can look at comfortably. Place all of your attention on that spot, and as you continue to do so, notice your breathing. After a while you may or may not notice that as you continue to look and focus, your peripheral vision has expanded and you are now more aware of what is to your left and right, as you keep all of your attention on that one spot. Once you have noticed your peripheral vision expand, or after a minute or so, lower your eyes to eye level and notice how you feel. Take a moment to describe how you feel immediately after carrying out this exercise.

_____

_____

_____

From experience finding a place of stillness and peace of mind whilst coaching is far more important than any other one factor, as it enables our intuitive wisdom to manifest at the appropriate time.

Given this stillness, this preparation for coaching, we realise that we are already at step 1 of the coaching process: building rapport with the client (see Figure 4.2).

Build rapport

Motivational maps and detailed personal history

Subconscious interventions: Present in the Moment

Goals and actions

Positive reinforcement and ongoing review

Figure 4.2 Five-step NLP intervention programme

We are not cluttering their minds with all our busy opinions and judgement calls; instead, we are ready to listen to them and build rapport.

Step 2 in our NLP programme we call Taking a Detailed Personal History. This includes a Motivational Map, so see Chapter 2 for more on relevant questions, but also additional intuitive questioning that arises in the moment.

Once we understand where the client is coming from, what the subconscious blocks are likely to be, then we can move to step 3.

Step 3 is the subconscious intervention to help the client have a self-evident experience of letting go of their subconscious blocks.

Step 4 is converting the understanding into action. In other words, tasking the client to complete a task or take first steps in an area where they are weak, and which builds appropriate confidence there. Clearly, preceding the actual action step is the need to write down the goal underpinning it; so, if we fear speaking in public, then we need a goal to express our intention to overcome it. Notice how in our model the goal setting is relegated to point 4 – it is deferred to allow the subconscious of client and coach to kick in more effectively.

Step 5 is then the positive reinforcement, monitoring of client progress, ongoing tasking and conversational coaching, which reviews and further positively impacts the client's situation, 'adversity', worldview aka 'beliefs' (to prevent slippage), and generally supportive moves by the coach. Ultimately, it leads to the celebration of success and achievement – look, so much has been done that before was thought impossible!

Building rapport and the NLP perspective

NLP takes as a given that communication is more than simply the words that we use. Alongside tonality there is volume, pace, pitch, tempo, rhythm – as well as other linguistic features[11] – of our speech, and then of course our body language. We have all probably heard at some point in our life that it is not what you say that is important, but how you say it!

'How' you say it is all about what is called Non-Verbal Communication (or NVC), which includes tone of voice and body language as two core components of the meaning that we convey to another. One of the weirdest things is when – and this happens frequently – the semantics (the words we use to express meaning) are contradicted by the NVC.[12] One of the key researchers here, Albert Mehrabian,[13] found that there was a disproportionate influence of NVC to words WHEN the situation was ambiguous. Ambiguous here usually means when someone is under stress, or is conflicted in some way, or does not wish to directly say what they think, for whatever reason. Clearly, too, NVC is more important when people are physically present than when they are over the phone, or communicating through e-mail.

Since work, negotiations, appraisals, tend to involve many ambiguous situations almost by their very nature, then understanding the importance of NVC is critical.

In NLP the focus is on observing changes of state (sensory acuity),[14] so that we can change tack or explore more deeply when we spot or notice a change of state with our client. And NVC is often a truer sign of how we feel than our words. It has two components, body language (which can represent some 55 per cent of our true meaning) and tone of voice (which can represent some 38 per cent). By way of contrast Verbal Communication – the words themselves – the semantics – can sometimes only represent only 7 per cent of what we mean! This, when you think about it, is astonishing (see Figure 4.3).

The body language reflects our intentions, attitudes, feelings; this, in Aristotelian[15] terms, is our ethos (from which we get the word 'ethics'). Our tone of voice reflects our state of mind and emotions; this, in Aristotelian terms, is our pathos (from which we get the word 'pathetic'). And words represent our meaning or semantics; this, in Aristotelian terms, is our logos (from which we get the word 'logical'). A summary is given in Figure 4.4.

We all like to think we are rational beings, but a moment's thought will, perhaps, persuade us that oftentimes we are influenced more by our emotions, or even more strongly by someone who is extremely 'credible' to us. This credibility issue – or ethos (which body language most often reveals) – is a leitmotif running through this book in the sense that what coaching is about is releasing one from erroneous, limiting and injurious self-beliefs that we have acquired throughout our lifetime. But where do the most powerful of these limiting beliefs come from, and why do we accept them? The answer should be clear: they come from our earliest years, and we accept them because the sources of them – our parents, carers and teachers – are massively 'credible' people; at least, they are *then*. So NLP pays attention not only to the words, but the shifts and 'paralanguage' that is NVC.

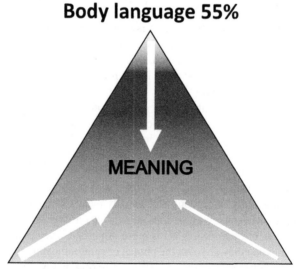

Figure 4.3 55–38–7 formula

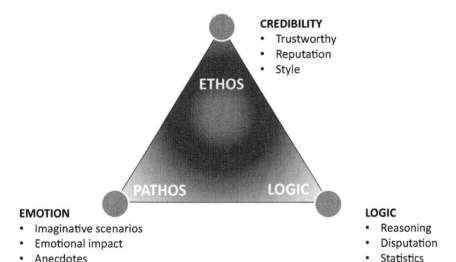

CREDIBILITY
- Trustworthy
- Reputation
- Style

ETHOS

PATHOS

LOGIC

EMOTION
- Imaginative scenarios
- Emotional impact
- Anecdotes

LOGIC
- Reasoning
- Disputation
- Statistics

Figure 4.4 Aristotle's three means of persuasion

ACTIVITY 4.3

Have you ever felt uncomfortable with someone and not known why? Try to remember the person, the incident, and recall how they stood or sat, their tone of voice. What about them jarred with you? How were you positioned?

Conversely have you ever felt immediately at ease with someone? Do the same exercise as for when you felt less comfortable. Chances are that if you felt at ease then you naturally adopted similar stances and seating positions as the other person.

When we consider the most optimum point at which two people are at ease with each other – are communicating in other words wholly, totally, and authentically – then without doubt it is when two people are in love. If we observe people who are romantically connected having a meal out together, then we find – as we do when they dance – that as one person leans forward so the other matches or mirrors their movement; conversely, when people are 'disconnected' or disconnecting their body language is mismatched or not mirroring.

Matching and mirroring is the process of adopting the same body language as the person whom you are communicating with. Sometimes this is done purely subconsciously; and it happens most times subconsciously – people get on and unbeknownst to themselves they are matching and mirroring each other's body language and speech patterns.[16] But in NLP we are seeking to deliberately utilise this phenomenon in order to increase rapport and therefore effective communication.

ACTIVITY 4.4

Is there anyone with whom you come into contact and *struggle*? Write their name down. Next time you meet them notice their body language. Specifically, notice if their natural posture is different from yours. Look for:

How they stand – straight, hunched, twisted, rigid, relaxed – how do you?
How they sit – leant forwards, backwards, centred, slumped, energised – how do you?
How they gesture, especially with their hands and head – how do you?

The aim is not to mirror them immediately, but gradually to adopt some of their forms, so that the process is subtle and non-obvious. Eventually, to be like them, so that they subconsciously feel comfortable with you.

ACTIVITY 4.5

Three key aspects of the voice that are relatively easy to match are:

Tone – what emotions does the tone reveal – professional neutrality, anger, sadness, fear?
Volume – are they typically loud, quiet or about average in their volume?
Tempo – or speed – do you find yourself hoping they'll get to the end of their sentence, or wishing they'd slow down?

Consider the contact with whom you struggled in **Activity 4.4**. Now reflect on their voice characteristics as per the three key aspects above. Aim, again, to gradually match their tone, or volume or tempo, or combination of these three aspects.

Now take one aspect – for example, the tone – and having matched them, see if you can – assuming the rapport has been established – change or vary your tone to one that you think is more beneficial for the discussion.

For example, to slowly switch from, say, a sad or upset tone to a more pro-fessionally neutral one. This process is called 'leading' in NLP. In fact, it reverses what you have begun: for you start with them leading you, as you match them, but then having established the rapport, they are more open to be led by you if indeed you choose to.

Intuitive questioning and the detailed personal history

One key NLP technique is called the Hierarchy of Ideas.[17] This is useful for improving communication between people with a different preference for detail. The Hierarchy of Ideas (see Figure 4.5) tells us that people range from:

EXTREME BIG PICTURE – being so big picture that often they don't really know what it is they want; they just have a vague concept, which they will recog-nise only when they see, hear, sense and experience it. People who are big picture tend to deal with abstract, vague concepts and these traits are more linked to sen-ior management and leadership than they are with technical expertise.

At the other end of the spectrum we have people who are very ...

DETAIL ORIENTED – that they almost appear to be talking a different language to us! Have you ever experienced that? Clearly, those at the extreme big picture end of the spectrum are speaking a very different language to those who are very detail oriented.

What the Hierarchy of Ideas does is provide us with a simple linguistic tech-nique that we can use to provide an antidote to the mismatch in level of detail. Communication can then occur at a level of detail that both parties understand; it also helps ensure that both parties have a clear understanding of the correct next steps.

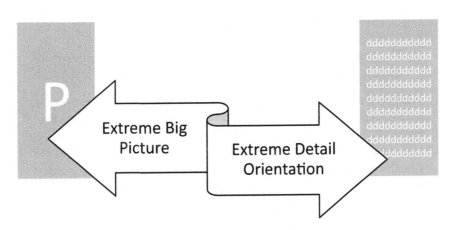

Figure 4.5 Big picture to detail orientation

In order to establish the hierarchy of ideas, we 'chunk'[18] down, or up, questions. Here is an example of **chunking down**:

A: *I'm unhappy!*
B: *What specifically are you unhappy about?*
A: *My husband said he wanted to play golf on Sunday!*
B: *What specifically about that has caused you to feel unhappy?*
A: *That means that he would rather play golf than spend time with me.*

Notice how with two chunking down questions we have gone from what we call a 'presenting' problem to the real reason that the person is unhappy.

In NLP when a client describes one thing and means another we call that a 'complex equivalence'[19]; and it is surprising how often we do it.

> *I'm unhappy – [may mean] – I have a problem – [which may mean] – this has nothing to do with work, though I am at work – [which may mean] – I cannot focus until you help me – [which may mean] – you are my boss/colleague, so you should help me – [which may mean] – please listen to me and empathise – [which may mean] – and so on ...*

What often appears trivial can be the 'presenting' of what is an underlying and serious issue; from a coaching perspective once a client can understand the associations that they are making in their mind, they can often see how irrational they are and how they might address them.

Case Study 4.1

The Chef – chunking down

CHEF: There is no communication around here!
BEVIS: Who specifically is not communicating with whom?
CHEF: *Long pause and uncomfortable body language* ... [then] It's Wendy; she just isn't talking to me!

Bevis here was the Chef's boss and Centre Manager. Previously, before NLP skills, if someone had come up with a statement like that, Bevis would have taken it personally and then quizzed people about communication! In this instance with a couple of questions, using the Chunking technique, what he actually established was that the problem was isolated to – the Chef and his wife working together! They were not communicating – this was solvable, and a lot easier to deal with than 'everyone' not communicating.

Chunking up is the reverse of chunking down. So we move, in the latter, from generalities to specifics, and in the former from specifics to generalities; and this too can be extremely useful. For example, when dealing with a difficult person or member of staff, chunking up can help both sides see how co-operating can lead to mutual advantage.

TEACHER (AGGRIEVED AT HAVING TO ATTEND AN EVENING PARENTS' MEET-
ING): Being here really is a waste of time.
HEADTEACHER: But you are helping your pupils by being here, James.
TEACHER: I fail to see how.
HEADTEACHER: It's not just about informing parents of progress, which reports do; it's enlisting their support.
TEACHER: How does that help?
HEADTEACHER: Well, for example, in support of our homework policy.
Why not ask them what they are doing to support the school's policy?
TEACHER: I suppose I could.
HEADTEACHER: We all want the best for the kids, don't we?

Here the Headteacher has moved the grievance of the teacher from a specific issue – attending a parents' evening – to the wider issue of getting the best for and out of the pupils. The Headteacher has chunked up! And for the teacher (or member of staff anywhere) who replied, 'I don't care about getting the best for the pupil' (or customer or client, etc.), then the game would be up.

Case Study 4.2

The Accountant – chunking up

One of Bevis's clients ran a successful accountancy practice, but was suffering from stress and overwork, which negatively impacted his health. He was striving to achieve a turnover target to sell his business. So Bevis asked him what the purpose of selling the business was; he got stuck! He had been so fixated on achievement – and the details – that he hadn't seen the bigger picture. So here we have chunking up. The conversation went like this.

BEVIS: What is the purpose of achieving £9xxx turnover?

CLIENT: To achieve a level of business that makes it attractive to sell!
BEVIS: What is the purpose of selling the business?
CLIENT: To realise £7xxx amount of capital?
BEVIS: What is the purpose for you of realising that capital level?
CLIENT: So I don't have to work so hard and I can be free to do what I want to do?
BEVIS: And for you what is the purpose of not working so hard and being free to do what you want?
CLIENT: So I can relax and feel good.
BEVIS: So can you now recognise that the purpose of achieving this, and in fact of anything, is to feel good?
CLIENT: *Long pause ... Yes, I can.*
BEVIS: So, do you feel good now, right now?
CLIENT: *Even longer pause and reflection ...*

This last sentence proved the emotional and lightbulb moment for the client; for suddenly their perception of all that they were doing changed. They realised – how long could they go on NOT feeling good in order for someday/one day to maybe feel good, and only IF they made that sale, and IF things turned out well? Indeed, they realised that they had to grasp feeling good now – in the present moment – and that their failure to do so was almost entirely responsible for their current stress and burnout.

This part of the process is called 'loosening the client's model of the world'. It appreciates that people actually project their problems outside of themselves. A key presupposition of NLP is PERCEPTION is PROJECTION[20]: We impose our beliefs onto the world and attempt to make the world conform to what we believe, rather than adapt our beliefs to what the world is, as it manifests itself to us.[21]

This issue of Hierarchy of Ideas and Chunking is also something that Motivational Maps has an angle on. This can be used as a complementary technique alongside the chunking questions, or an anticipatory view of what is likely to emerge from the questioning. Maps give insight, for they also reveal Learning Styles (see Figure 4.6).

We need to keep in mind that Motivational Maps is polysemous[22]; and most people do not have their top three motivators all in one category of R or A or G; they are mixed. And even when they do have them all of one type, that still leaves room for other factors to influence them. That said, however, we can still see how

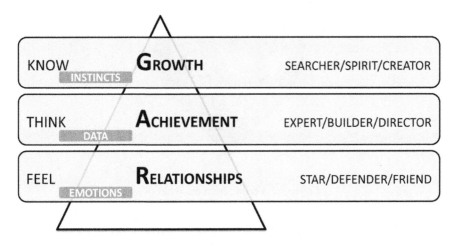

Figure 4.6 Feel–Think–Know learning styles

the Maps can help anyone to 'shift' their perspective by being able to see their own motivational driver (see Figures 4.7–4.9).

Clients with Relationship type motivators are more likely to have a past tense orientation, especially regarding how things worked before. They will want a strong emotional commitment from the coach, and they are best influenced when propositions are filtered through the mechanisms of stories, examples, descriptions and anecdotes; these open the door, as it were, for them, as they affect their feelings.

But with clients who have Achievement type motivators predominantly, who tend to be in the present tense, and are asking what works now, these are much more detail and analytically oriented. Hence, they want hard data from the coach and they are best influenced when propositions are filtered through the mechanisms of data, statistics, and research; these open the door for them, as they affect their thinking.

Finally, clients with the Growth type motivators predominantly tend to be future tense oriented and like imagining what might work in future; these are much more big picture and vision centred. Imagining their vision and checking in with themselves subconsciously that this feels good! They want to know how what is happening now will link to their ability to actualise their future vision, the correlation which can open the door to their imagination! This begins the process by which they access their intuition, or sense of knowing (what to do next).

The connection, then, with NLP and language is the appropriate use of language to include metaphor and the appropriate shift from detail (A) to big picture (G) and back again.

Figure 4.7 Feeling from the Heart (R)

ACTIVITY 4.6

Review your Map profile now. Are you dominantly R, A, G, or a mixture? If you were or are coaching yourself, how is it best to persuade yourself? Do you like examples of good practice? Or, do you prefer working through numbers and doing the analysis? Or, do straightforward facts speak to your condition? Or is it a combination? Often people discover that they have a primary preference and a secondary back-up style. In dealing with other people it is important to realise that it is the third 'mode' – the one we don't tend to use – that is our Achilles' heel, for we tend not to adopt it on those people for whom it is primary.

But let's look now at another example of this DETAIL TO BIG PICTURE.[23]

Sometimes, in a meeting or on a project, the team are working with such detail that other members within the team cannot understand what it is they are saying. This lack of understanding can entirely derail the meeting for the level of detail within the project may not be available yet.

SAM: I can't agree to authorising that training as we don't have enough detail to proceed.

VIJAY: What is the purpose of the training?

SAM: To enable the programmers to improve the software's security.

VIJAY: Are we agreed that improving security is value-add for the client?

SAM: Well, yes. We need to do that …

VIJAY: Then, Sam, can we all agree to move forward with the training with the purpose of improving the software's security and we can ensure the details become filled in later?

The ability to ask someone what the purpose is can be so powerful in coaching, since for so many it is easy to lose sight of *why* they are doing *what* they are doing.

Figure 4.8 Thinking from the Head (A)

NLP takes the view that subconscious Limiting Beliefs are at the root of poor or non-performance; indeed, of failure itself. Typical limiting beliefs that cause big issues for clients include ...

"I'm not good enough"
"I don't deserve to be successful"
"I don't deserve big money"
"I'm not worthy of being loved"

The problem with these beliefs being subconscious is that they are outside of our conscious awareness, so how do we find them? The answer is by a kind of observational logic! The beliefs are causes; but outcomes are symptoms. If we look at the 'results' in our life and work backwards, we see what the underlying beliefs must be. And then as we frame them in our minds, we 'feel' the truth of it. The coach helps us here by asking good questions that pinpoint these 'symptoms'.

ACTIVITY 4.7

What results in your life are you unhappy about at the moment?
   What a great and simple question!
   Consider results in the three areas of Relationships (R) – family, friends, social; Achievement (A) – work, career, mission; and Growth (G) – your own personal development and learning.
   Write down your answers.

_____
_____
_____

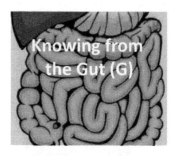

Figure 4.9 Knowing from the Gut (G)

All results that are disappointing to you will have negative emotions from past events attached to them. Such as:

ANGER (linked to frustration)
SADNESS (linked with disappointment)
FEAR (linked with anxiety)
HURT (linked with low mood)
GUILT (linked with regret)

What memories do you have which still hold negative emotions for you? Write them down here and notice the feeling in the body as you do so. If an emotion needs to release itself, then allow it to do so. Many people have been subconsciously putting a lid on their emotions, and this over time is fruitless, as they will at some point come to the boil.

_____

_____

_____

In Chapter 2 we looked at the Seven Success Elements of our life. We have extended this model to include typical limiting beliefs in all of the Seven Element categories, and include what antidote or healthier beliefs might prove to be:

ACTIVITY 4.8

Having done the previous Activities, and now reviewing these examples of limiting beliefs, choose two or three that you feel are especially relevant to you. Choose to replace your limiting beliefs with their corresponding empowering beliefs. Write the empowering beliefs down on paper; make them a mantra that you regularly repeat to yourself.

SUCCESS ELEMENT		
1 SELF ESTEEM	**EMPOWERING BELIEFS**	**LIMITING BELIEFS**
	Every challenge I face stimulates my inner confidence and my inner strengths.	I am powerless.
		I am not worthy of love and respect.
	I love and accept myself unconditionally.	There is something basically wrong with me.
	I am very special. I like who I am and feel good about myself.	I am inadequate and insecure.

SUCCESS ELEMENT		
2 ENERGY	**EMPOWERING BELIEFS**	**LIMITING BELIEFS**
	I am vibrant, healthy and alive.	My body and health are out of balance.
	My immune system is strong, healthy and powerful.	I am in embarrassingly bad condition.
	I look forward to exercising and staying youthful in my mind, body and spirit.	Getting sick and illnesses are inescapable.

Figure 4.10 Empowering and limiting beliefs for the Seven Success Elements: (i) Self Esteem, (ii) Energy, (iii) Quality Relationships, (iv) Wealth, (v) Meaning, (vi) Growth, (vii) Self Awareness

SUCCESS ELEMENT		
3 QUALITY RELATIONSHIPS	**EMPOWERING BELIEFS**	**LIMITING BELIEFS**
	The more I love and appreciate myself, the more love I have to give others.	People really upset me.
	I am worthy of love and respect.	Relationships never work out for me. You can't rely on people.
	People are good and can be trusted.	

SUCCESS ELEMENT		
4 WEALTH	**EMPOWERING BELIEFS**	**LIMITING BELIEFS**
	I have a strong belief in my ability to manifest financial prosperity.	I can't earn enough money to support my lifestyle.
	I have released all fear and desperation around money.	I do not have the confidence to create wealth and abundance.
	I deserve financial prosperity and abundance.	Making money is a struggle. I can never get ahead.

Figure 4.10 (Continued)

By placing awareness on the emotions, notice that *one* is not the emotion; the disassociation from ourselves means the emotion does not take us over. If for whatever reason it does, then this is a sure sign that more help and support[24] are needed.

One key premise from NLP is that your subconscious mind's primary directive is to protect you! If, therefore, we experience significant negative emotion around an event, or series of events, the subconscious adapts its learnings, beliefs and emotions linked with them to help protect you from it or them. What this means in practical terms is that the mind has a defence mechanism that can shield us from harm; but

SUCCESS ELEMENT	EMPOWERING BELIEFS	
5 MEANING		LIMITING BELIEFS
	I look forward to taking on new challenges.	It's best to play safe.
	I think for myself and I stand up for my ideas.	Things always go wrong – it's Murphy's Law.
	I am fully in charge of my own life.	It's not what you know but who you know.

SUCCESS ELEMENT	EMPOWERING BELIEFS	
6 GROWTH		LIMITING BELIEFS
	I can handle whatever comes my way.	I feel empty and weak.
	I deserve acknowledgment and advancement for my job performance.	I am trapped by my past.
	I am continually discovering new qualities, talents, and abilities about myself.	It's dangerous taking risks.

Figure 4.10 (Continued)

sometimes this can come at a painful or unacceptable price. For example, we go into denial about pain and certain experiences, and we filter 'out' part of reality that we don't want to accept. This, then, becomes a sort of blind spot in our life; we go on excluding part of our reality, and this can have dangerous, emotional consequences.

One non-therapeutic way of breaking through these negative emotions is an extension of what we talked about earlier with stillness or presence. Bevis noticed, even as he first began practising as an NLP coach, that some clients – extraordinarily – seemed, after they had had a detailed personal history taken and

SUCCESS ELEMENT	EMPOWERING BELIEFS	LIMITING BELIEFS
7 SELF AWARENESS	I see depth and possibilities in myself I never saw before.	Life is always the same and quite boring actually.
	I honour my body and listen to its signals.	I know it all.
	I listen carefully to other people's opinions.	You can't tell me what to do.

BEFORE any intervention occurred, to be able to heal themselves. It seemed that conscious awareness of the issues, together with courage and acceptance, was enough to heal deeply.

What this constitutes is the idea when we are truly PRESENT IN THE MOMENT no negative emotion can exist, for all our negative emotions only ever live in the past, or in the future (when the mind drifts from the present, creates associations between the past and our expectations about the future). So whilst this is not a book on how to meditate, clearly meditation is important, and Activities 4.1 and 4.2 are the start of becoming centred in the mind. Additionally, Buddhism identifies Five Hindrances[25] to meditation, which are worth noting and commenting on. These are Sensual Craving, Ill-will or Hatred, Sloth, Worry, Doubt or Wavering. It is important to recognise these feelings as they arise; for without self-awareness we cannot counter these tendencies in us.

Sensual Craving means I WANT MORE. The false belief is that mere sensory indulgence can extirpate inner pain. If only I had 'X' everything would be alright. Examples of sensual craving range from clinical addictions at one extreme down to activities like drinking coffee or retail therapy.

Ill-Will means I REJECT MORE. Mind chooses to focus on negative aspects of a person, object, situation or idea. Ill-will involves the wish to wipe out or be rid of somebody, something, or some idea perceived as preventing one's happiness or contentment. Ill-will ranges from paranoid states and utter malice down to minor everyday irritations.

Sloth means I DON'T CARE. Mind rejects the present moment by resorting to laziness, indifference, inactivity, sleep and daydreams. The mind wants to be relaxed and comfortable rather than paying attention to the processes it is attempting to undertake.

Worry means I NEED PERFECTION. Here mind is attempting to organise, control, and rehearse the future. The hindrance ranges from blind panic and anxiety states down to obsessive planning at inappropriate times. The mind is ceaselessly restless.

Doubt means I LACK FAITH. Doubt in oneself or in others or in 'God'. Doubt leads to speculation and questions but no real regard for the answers. Often, 'always learning but never coming to knowledge of the truth' is their condition. Questions lead them only to increased confusion.

In our experience the 80/20 Rule (the Pareto Principle) we looked at in Chapter 3 applies here. Most people in other words find that one or two of these hindrances are their particular issue, and account for most of their distraction and inability to remain in the present.

ACTIVITY 4.9

Which of these five hindrances do you think you suffer from? What beliefs underpin the hindrance? What counter-beliefs can you put in place to help you resist the hindrance? How will you increase your ability to meditate and stay in the present moment?

The general rules for overcoming a hindrance are:

a   recognise it to be a hindrance;
b   accept and experience the hindrance next time it occurs; don't struggle, but note its effect on your mental state and the feeling within the body;
c   experience the 'negative' aspects of the hindrance and choose a different response.

Thus, increasing self-awareness is at the heart of our ability to grow, learn and transform.

Finally, it wouldn't be right to leave NLP without attempting to define it, which many NLP Practitioners, Master Practitioners and Trainers often still struggle with, so let's leave you with some simple guidance and Bevis's favourite descriptions of NLP:

Neuro – Developing a greater understanding of the mind to help you and others.
Linguistic – Using that enhanced knowledge of the mind and its workings to develop greater flexibility of nonverbal and verbal communication.
Programming – Learning the coaching and therapeutic tools of NLP to help people overcome subconscious blocks.

In short, NLP is an instruction manual for the mind! NLP helps you to both consciously and subconsciously focus on the outcome you want!

Summary

1   The four pillars of NLP are clarity and congruency of goals, sensory acuity, behavioural flexibility, and the ability to build strong relationships.

2   NLP assists coaching through enhancing rapport, the ability to ask intuitive questions and help the client to achieve clarity of direction.

3   The skill of the NLP coach is to gain control over their state, or the ability to be still with their clients, which enhances intuition and the ability to access unconscious resources.

4   NLP coaching involves five key steps: building rapport, taking a detailed personal history, assisting the client in overcoming subconscious blocks, the setting of action steps and tasks, and then positive re-enforcement and confidence building.

5   Face to face body language and tone of voice can be more important than the actual words you use when influencing.

6   Superior rapport can be achieved through matching and mirroring body language, tonality and the type of language your client is using.

7   In organisations each individual will have a different level of comfort with detail, and many misunderstandings stem from these preferences for different levels of detail.

8   Subconscious limiting beliefs play a large part in our ability to succeed or fail; and the subconscious mind's prime directive is to protect us. Often emotional blocks, including Fear, Anger, Sadness, Hurt or Guilt, are our subconscious mind trying to protect us from emotional pain linked to a past event or trauma.

9   Understanding the Five Buddhist Hindrances can help overcome negative mental states.

Notes

1   Richard Bandler and John Grinder, *Frogs into Princes*, Real People Press (1979).

2   Bob Bates, *The Little Book of Big Coaching Models*, Pearson (2015).

3   Nigel MacLennan, *Coaching and Mentoring*, Gower (1995).

4   A wonderful expression of this is from the great seventeenth century philosopher Blaise Pascal when he said, "The heart has its reasons that reason does not know about" - *The Pensées* (1669).

5   The most popular and best-selling account of this idea over the last 15 years has been Eckhart Tolle's book, *The Power of Now*, Yellow Kite (2001).

6   Meditation is the process and the objective by which self-awareness is maximised. This leads to the interesting reflection that altered brain wave patterns - not the everyday beta brain wave patterns (c. 13-35 Hz) - are intimately connected with developing self-awareness.

7   Which they call a meta model. A fascinating and detailed account, beyond the scope of this book, is given in Richard Bandler's *Guide to Trance Formation*, Health Communications (2008).

8   The Collective Unconscious was a phrase coined by the famous psychologist C. G. Jung in his book, *The Archetypes and the Collective Unconscious*, Routledge (1959). For our purposes we regard all these phrases as synonymous.

9 There are four major brain or mind states that we encounter on a daily basis: Beta, Alpha, Theta and Delta. According to Dr Lee Pulos, *Training the Mind's Eye*, Nightingale Conant (1993), beta is the range of 13-35 Hertz and represents our everyday alert state; alpha is 8-12 Hertz and is when we meditate; theta is 4-8 Hertz and is when we receive dreams, images and healing; and finally delta at 0.5-4 Hertz is when we are in deep sleep. Thus at least twice a day - going into and coming out of sleep - we pass through all these brain wave frequencies. For more on brain wave frequencies see Chapter 8.

10 Hakalua is a technique NLP borrowed from the Hawaiian spiritual and healing practice called Huna (which means 'secret'). One meaning of Hakalua is, "To stare at as in meditation and to allow to spread out" - http://bit.ly/2un27pb. In NLP it is called The Learning State. See also: *Huna: A Beginner's Guide*, Enid Hoffman, Whitford Press (1981).

11 Harry Alder and Beryl Heather also list timbre and phrases in their *NLP in 21 Days*, Piatkus (1998).

12 "When there are inconsistencies between attitudes communicated verbally and posturally, the postural component should dominate in determining the total attitude that is inferred" - Albert Mehrabian, *Nonverbal Communication*, Aldine Transaction (2007).

13 Albert Mehrabian, *Silent Messages*, Belmont (1971).

14 Andy Smith, *Practical NLP 3: Sensory Acuity and Rapport*, Kindle Edition (2014).

15 Aristotle in his *Art of Rhetoric* identified three primary methods of persuasion - or communication if you will. The Ethos appealed to the character or credibility of the persuader. Pathos appealed to emotion, whereas Logos appealed to logic and reason.

16 Harry Alder, ibid., suggests six areas where matching is important: body language, voice (which we are looking at), but also language and thinking style, beliefs and values, experience, and most subtly, breathing.

17 Harry Alder, ibid.

18 Sometimes called 'Stepping'. Steve Andreas and Charles Faulkner, *NLP: The New Technology of Achievement*, Nicholas Brealey (1996).

19 Harry Alder, ibid., defines it this way: "Two statements that are considered to mean the same thing, e.g. 'He is not looking at me, so he is not listening to what I say'".

20 This presupposition is not only found within NLP, but, for example, A Course in Miracles holds a similar view: *Foundation for Inner Peace*, Arkana, new edition (1989).

21 This idea of our conforming to the world is represented in belief systems such as the Tao Te Ching, Buddhism, and Hinduism where concepts like 'maya' represents the illusions that we ferociously grasp and are attached to, but which mislead us into grave error. We lose our 'way'.

22 Polysemous comes from the Greek meaning 'of many senses', or 'several meanings' in other words. As we like to say, Maps are contextual, and meanings can vary according to context.

23 The key experts in this field, upon which NLP was modelled, are Virginia Satir and Milton Erickson. Erickson once famously said: "I think my client should have the freedom to do exactly what I'm telling them, in any way they like". His style was extremely non-directive. Cited by Tad James and Lorraine Flores, *Hypnosis: A Comprehensive Guide*, Crown House Publishing (2000).

24 From an advanced NLP perspective, we would recommend Time Line Therapy techniques, which were devised by Tad James; however, other psychological approaches such as counselling or psychotherapy can be effective.

25 *Buddhism: The Plain Facts*, Robert Mann and Rose Youd, Aukana Trust (2004).

5 Unblocking two barriers to success: Time and Money

We have throughout been emphasising the importance of developing self-awareness, and from that process gaining greater clarity about what it is we are trying to achieve. However, once we understand what we are trying to do inevitably we also become aware that there are blockages – barriers – in our way that, as things currently stand, prevent this happening. Our job is to understand what these barriers are and then to find out how to remove them from our path. The coach has another crucial role, then: he or she has enabled the client to get clarity on where the destination leads, but now the coach has to help the client understand what needs to be done to get there. That is, how does the client demolish the barriers that are preventing access to the 'promised land', which is where the client wishes to go?

To be clear: the client has a clearly defined outcome, with a sense of what that sounds, looks and feels like, and which is compelling to the subconscious mind. There is also an appropriate time frame. The time frame acts as an accelerator; without it, there is drift and no urgency: As the famous conductor Leonard Bernstein said: "to achieve great things, two things are needed: a plan, and not quite enough time[1]"! With these in place we can begin to explore what the potential barriers to the achievement of those outcomes could be.

ACTIVITY 5.1

What are the top three barriers to success?

When you consider the barriers to performance and achievement, what do you think the three most commonly identified perceptions of obstacles to achievement are? (See Figure 5.1.)

In our view, based upon the hundreds of people we have coached and the experience of the coaches we have trained, the three key and classic barriers

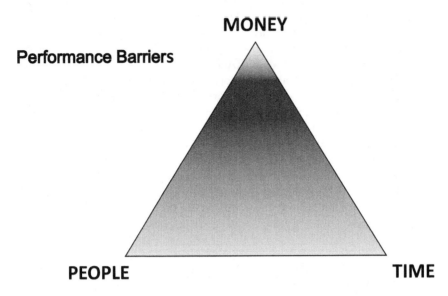

MONEY

Performance Barriers

PEOPLE   **TIME**

Figure 5.1 Three performance barriers

to achievement are: TIME or MONEY or PEOPLE[2] (or a combination!). Yet in truth these can never be the real obstacles to achievement. Why? First, because nobody is ever really in a unique situation that has never been done before: other people faced your barriers in similar, if not identical circumstance, so why were they enabled to push through and succeed, despite – like you – having no time or money or people connections? Second, because on examination we find that the principle of the self-fulfilling prophecy[3] is true; what you expect, you tend to get. The real battle is not external factors such as time, money or people, but the internal ones: factors such as our belief systems, especially our belief system about ourselves.[4] This is often called the self-concept. If you are *confident*[5] and *have belief*, then much more is possible. Holding the expectation that one can succeed not only mobilises the latent, subconscious powers, but it also does something else: it shifts us emotionally, and one critical shift is that it drives out fear – the fear of failure and the fear of rejection especially.

   If this sounds rather remote and touchy-feely, then consider this. In our right mind – which is to say, our fearless mind – we can objectively consider any barrier such as our lack, say, of money and realise the blindingly obvious: that you can in this day and age borrow the money, find investment and investors, and pursue your goal. This is not to say it's easy, particularly when this is the first time you have attempted it, but it is possible.

So, the real barrier to performance is not money but *sufficient confidence and specific belief*(s) and we will explore later in this chapter how to overcome and improve both these intangible areas.

However, before that it is worth seeing how the three barriers in a way are analogous to the Motivational Maps' RAG model (see Figure 5.2).

This is not to claim an absolute correspondence between the Map profile and the particular set of problems a client may have or encounter. But clearly, people issues are relationship issues and deep relationships are invariably grounded in our past; achievement issues from the point of view of business are generally condensed into the form of money or lack thereof, and achievement happens in the present tense, the now; and time is a critical ingredient of all growth and growth always has a future orientation. It might be useful to consider, when practically coaching the client, whether or not their dominant issue is in an area where their RAG score is lowest or especially weak.

ACTIVITY 5.2

Coach yourself! Rank order the issues of Time, Money, and People (TMP) for yourself. Which one creates the most problems for you? Now review your own Motivational Map profile. Which of the RAG triad are you dominant in? Is there a correlation between your RAG strength and your TMP issue? What are the implications of this for you?

With these points in mind, and leaving people barriers for Chapter 6, as they are generally considered the most difficult of all to deal with, we can focus now on TIME! How does time act as a barrier to performance?

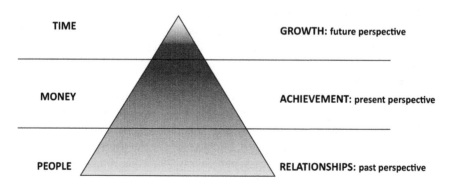

Figure 5.2 Possible alignment of Time, Money, and People with RAG

You will have heard it said that we all have the same amount of time in the day, those 24 short hours! So why is it that some people are able to achieve so much in seemingly so little time, whereas other people struggle to get things off the ground?

The key issue here is, as elsewhere, our beliefs. We are constantly in a struggle in which we believe that we do not have enough time. If we believe that we do not have enough time, then we know that that will become self-fulfilling; furthermore, it will also produce great stress and anxiety in us as we anticipate that we will fail. Yet we have seen from the Pareto Principle that 80 per cent of our time is concerned with the 'trivial many' and not the 'vital few'[6] things we should – or might – be doing. In other words, there is always lots of time available: the 80 per cent of our time, whether at work or home, which we are using, or misusing for the 'trivial many' activities. Hence, what this comes down to really is: prioritisation – an accurate assessment of what is important in our life and work, and a focus on increasing the amount of time we spend there. Maybe, then, our 20 per cent on the vital few becomes 30 per cent of our time. Note what that does: it actually increases the amount of time we spend on what is important by 50 per cent! Would that make a difference? Well, if you said you had 50 per cent more money to invest in a project, then that usually would be significant. And let's not stop at 30 per cent. Suppose you made that 40 per cent, then that would double your time on what is important and still leave you 60 per cent of your time to indulge in 'trivial many' activities. Therefore, the key thing here is to audit yourself.[7] Work out what you need to do more of, to do less of, and what stays the same.

ACTIVITY 5.3

We have extended the usefulness of this tool for coaching to include not only DOING, but also HAVING and BEING as both these additional states can waste or refresh time for us. If we are, for example, constantly BEING angry or upset, then we are not in a position to be productive; if we are constantly in a position of HAVING arguments with others, the same applies.

Without judging, just jot down all your ideas about your life or work currently. What do you want to have less of, do more of, or continue being? People who complete this usually find there is a pattern that emerges. We often find, for example, that when people review the use of their time that their issue is either predominantly about what they are 'doing' or 'having' or 'being', and so is not equally spread across all three categories. Of course, this applies as much to 'less' as it does to 'more' – we may be doing/having/being too little in certain key areas and too much in irrelevant areas. There may not be, but is there a pattern? Effectively, this coaching tool enables you – and your client – to stop for a moment and think seriously about what is happening, and what truly is important; it helps sort priorities so you and they can gain more control, which is very motivating.

	STOP	LESS	CONTINUE	MORE	START
BEING					
DOING					
HAVING					

Figure 5.3 Stop–Start review

But let's be clear: time is perplexing and fascinating to everybody. We think we know what it is, but there is a sense in which it is like some giant from Greek mythology who we constantly have to wrestle with and seem never able to defeat. Only perpetual vigilance (so do the Stop–Start review often!) suffices to come anywhere near overcoming this giant. Philip Zimbardo[8] claims that the word 'time' itself is the most popular noun (based on Internet searches) in the English language. Yet for all our inability to get to grips with 'Time' and defeat it in an absolute sense, we need to be aware that our powers are far greater than we traditionally think; even here, even with an enemy of this stature and seemingly relentless power. And again, we come back to the issue – the critical issue – of what we believe.

As we coach ourselves and others, it is as well to remind ourselves of the famous research that Professor Ellen Langer[9] conducted in 1979. In a week long experiment a group of 75-year-old men were isolated on a retreat camp in which everything – their clothes, their décor, their furniture, their food, their music, their radio broadcasts and newspapers – replicated how it was in 1959 when they were only 55 years old. Before they entered the retreat they were assessed on their physiological and psychological condition. In only one week of immersion in the 'life' of how they were living 20 years ago the conditions led to some astonishing results: on all markers they improved. For example, average eye sight, memory retention, physical strength, all improved. And when independent people who were not privy to the experiment were asked to guess the ages of the men from pictures before and after the experiment, the men on average were rated three years younger than when they arrived! Experiencing their past in such a vivid manner enabled them to believe they were younger, and so they became younger!! Astonishing, or what?

The implications of this are very similar to those of the placebo effect[10]: If people believe that a harmless pill or medical intervention is doing them good or healing them, the belief alone can sometimes be enough to effect the cure. These facts consistently disturb the scientific types who like tidy explanations, want to control life, and generally won't accept any 'fact' that isn't approved by science, or more precisely, scientism. But the reality – and the facts – all point to the power of belief to be able to, metaphorically, move mountains: the mountains, or the blocks and barriers in our life. Henry Ford put it this way[11]: "If you think you can do a thing or think you can't do a thing, you're right".

To help you reframe the time issue in your life, the ABCDE[12] model can be extremely useful. We will use the ABCDE method on the time issue, but the tool can be used on any other issue – such as money and people – too. Essentially, the ABCDE model is a cognitive behavioural tool that provides a five-step process that enables individuals (and coaches to help individuals) to re-think, and so re-frame, and so re-believe, what they normally assume. In this way, too, it enables individuals to stop reacting and to start responding far more effectively; and it does this by controlling our self-talk – our own internal dialogue – and turning on its positive tap.

The five steps of the ABCDE model in altering how you believe[13] and feel about a barrier are:

A is for **Adversity** – identify or define the block or barrier or 'adversity' encountered

 e.g. there's not enough time to complete my work

B is for **Belief** – note your thoughts and interpretation about the adversity

 e.g. a. I just have too much work to do; OR b. I can never get organised; OR c. I am not as efficient/effective as other people; OR, d. etc.

C is for **Consequences** – recognise what the consequences of your belief are

 e.g. for Belief a. feelings of I can't cope, feelings of I may as well give up, feelings of what's the point?

D is for **Dispute** – the negative belief with alternative evidence and better ideas

 e.g. for Belief a. i. when I plan my day in advance I find I get a better response; OR, ii. I could easily limit time spent on processing too many trivial emails and that would free me up a lot; OR, iii. I am good at organising my holiday itineraries and I can use those skills here.

E is for **Energy** – which is generated when we feel – that is, through believing – we can overcome the adversity we have initially experienced

 e.g. for Belief a. i. I'll feel better if I write out my plan for the day the night before I go to work; OR, ii. I'll limit my time spent on emails to 1 hour a day, and do them towards the end of the afternoon, so I am fresh to do my best work in the morning; OR, iii. I will set aside 1 day a week for a month to overhaul my working space, including my computer folders and directories, to make it easier for me to access the tools I need to be effective.

Clearly, these are just examples but the principle remains the same. When you reframe a barrier or what we are calling here an 'adversity' and realise that the beliefs about it are more destructive to your peace of mind and effectiveness than the adversity itself, and hence you reframe the situation in this way, there is a massive surge of energy, because you have found your hope – you believe you can cope, you are self-efficacious, and so your self-esteem is boosted.

ACTIVITY 5.4

We are looking at time as the barrier here. So go through the five-step process yourself with that in mind. But if you feel that time is not an 'adversity' to you personally, then try it as a run-through example, and afterwards choose your own adverse situation and run through this process again; it could then be about money, which we are coming onto, or even a person or people, which we deal with in Chapter 6.

Controlling your self-talk through the ABCDE Model

A – My adversity is I DO NOT HAVE ENOUGH TIME TO DO WHAT I WANT ...

B – I believe...

C – I feel..

D – Evidence to the contrary...

E – My energy level is...

Note how you feel at the end of the exercise if you have done it sincerely.

ACTIVITY 5.5

Now find a partner – could be a friend or colleague, or if you are a coach, then a client – and work as a pair on exactly the same ABCDE model as in Activity 5.4. Use another 'adversity' and this time go through the process for one of you with the other prompting and asking for greater clarification. Pay particular attention to DISPUTE – finding evidence to the contrary – as actively and energetically establishing that one's original beliefs are false is vital to the process.

If you have done Activities 5.4 and 5.5 fully, then it should be clear that it is possible to have a clear goal that feels right for you, and yet simultaneously to become aware of how your current priorities and focus could potentially be revealing a subconscious 'adversity' to your achieving what you want. To demonstrate this point here is Bevis's true story.

Case study 5.1

Bevis's story

At the start of my coaching career, trying to get my fledgling business off the ground, my coach offered to elicit my subconscious business beliefs to shed some light on potential barriers to its development.

He repeatedly asked me: "So in the context of your work what is important to you now?" After an hour there were a list of words on the flip chart in front of me; some were obvious, some less so. We tried prioritising the top ten in rank order. The coach then tested me with questions such as, "So, if you could only have one of x or y, which would you choose?"

This proved a painful and difficult process. Finally, when we had established them, my coach still seemed quizzical and asked if anything was missing?

"Nope", I said, confident that they truly were the most important things to me in my work.

Suffice to say, my coach came back several times, prodding and poking me verbally – was there anything missing? And I just couldn't get it – couldn't see it.

Finally, my coach gave up trying to get me to realise for myself what he could see plain as day. He said, "So, do you not think focusing on money might be important for you to run a successful coaching and training company?" The proverbial light bulb went on! Not only was money not in my top 10 current work values, it wasn't even on the flipchart of the 64 beliefs that had come up through the process. It seemed that money wasn't at all even on my subconscious radar; but he was right: if I was to run my own business I would need to pay more attention to and focus on the practicalities of money!

It did not surprise me that money was not on my radar, given my background. But if I was going to make a successful go at the career change I was planning, then I would need to change my subconscious beliefs, my priorities, or put more simply my career motivators! Only that would enable me to make the journey from Leisure Centre Manager to business entrepreneur and coaching expert.

This realisation – this light bulb moment – that Bevis had is crucial for all of us if we want to perform and achieve, if we want to surf for success, if we want surmount the dangerous reefs and shoals that are barely visible to us as we move forward. These are the barriers – adversities – that we need to surface, confront and redefine.

If we persist in remaining unaware of the potential subconscious issues, we are likely to struggle to achieve our desired outcomes. But with that awareness, we can:

a)   consciously work to pay more attention to the area not naturally in our awareness; and

b)   if necessary work with a coach to reconfigure our beliefs, to raise the profile, as it were, of one particular belief[14] or motivator to be more important than it currently is; and

c)   use Motivational Maps to ascertain some of the key areas of concern that might be affecting us.

ACTIVITY 5.6

Ask yourself in the context of your work/business/career what is important to you NOW?

Write down all the words that spring to mind. Aim for at least 50! And if you run out of ideas, don't quit, but pause and ask yourself the same question again. Give this process at least three goes.

Once you have your list of words, circle the ten most important. Choose at least 9 and a maximum of 12. Now that you have this list quickly prioritise the list 1–9/12. Double check the order. Ask yourself if you could only have one of the things in your current top two (in your work) which would it be? If you need to change the order because of your answers, then do so. Continue to check all the way through your list so that you are as confident as you can be that these are your top work values in the right sequence.

ACTIVITY 5.7

You now have your top beliefs. But how do they align with your goals? (See Figure 5.4). Do they match? Are there any incongruences? And, if you continue to focus on these beliefs in the priority order that they are in will that support the relationships, the personal growth that you desire, as well as the achievement or career you want? Re-examine the goals you created in Chapter 2.

My top 3 goals are:	My top 3 motivators are:	My top 3 beliefs are:
1	1	1
2	2	2
3	3	3

Figure 5.4 Top three goals and top three beliefs

To help you consider whether your goals and beliefs align, ask yourself: does this belief or motivator help me achieve this specific goal? Three simple examples might be:

> Goal: To achieve financial independence.
> Motivator – Builder motivator low?/Belief – 'Money doesn't grow on trees'[15]
> Goal: To become go-to authority in sector.
> Motivator – Expert motivator low?/Belief – 'I did really badly at school'
> Goal: To become key team member
> Motivator – Spirit motivator high?/Belief – 'I don't get on with people very well'

Now consider the following questions. If your goals and beliefs align, good. But

A. If not, what is the number one area where you will need to focus to help you achieve your goal?
B. Which belief(s) will you need to pay *less* attention to in order to achieve your goal?
C. How will you ensure on a weekly basis that attention is placed upon A above?
D. How can you ensure that attention is taken away from B? What decision needs to be made, what action needs to be taken, what do you need to stop doing?

Now re-visit Figure 5.3 and the Stop–Start review in the light of this further analysis of your own position. What more do you need to do? Commit to action.

Case study 5.2

Daniel's story – his dilemma

Daniel is the manager of a construction firm, which he built from scratch over three decades. Now in his fifties, he was concerned about his balance of life. Over a coffee and informal chat, he admitted that he felt like his PA was running his life, and that he knew that he did not want to have

his current lifestyle in five years, yet he didn't know how to stop. We casually suggested he may want to complete a Motivational Map to potentially
shine some light on the issues and this is what came back as the coach
report (see Figure 5.5).

We now need to dig into a deep understanding of how to read a Motivational Map through its numbers. To do this you need to understand that:

a.   Every individual has all 9 motivators in their profile but at different
     levels of intensity;
b.   The maximum intensity is 40 points and the minimum is 0 points;
     this records the strength of a motivator set against the strength of the
     other 8;
c.   The PMA score measures the satisfaction the client is experiencing
     from the motivator at that moment in time – which generally is a sta-
     ble number – and is out of 10 maximum satisfaction, and 1 minimum;

Analysis for Daniel: Raw Results

Motivator	Score	PMA Score / 10
Builder	28	9
Spirit	26	4
Searcher	24	9
Director	24	8
Expert	19	9
Star	18	9
Creator	14	6
Defender	14	9
Friend	13	9
PMA Score	75%	
Cluster Importance		
Relationship (R)	25%	
Achievement (A)	39%	
Growth (G)	36%	

Figure 5.5 Daniel's Map numbers

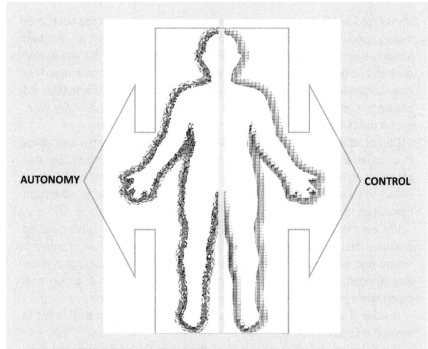

AUTONOMY   CONTROL

Figure 5.6 Daniel motivationally divided

d. Taking, then, the actual motivator score, 20 (out of 0–40 range) rep-
    resents the tipping point – higher than 20 equals a score that has
    traction for the individual; below 20 equals a score that indicates the
    motivator is not something one wants.

Considering Daniel's scores, we see that there are actually four
motivators – Builder, Spirit, Searcher, and Director – all well above
the 20 number and quite closely scored with a range of only 4 points
(28–24). So, when we sat to debrief him, Daniel appeared to see,
especially around the Director (desire for control) and his Spirit (desire
for autonomy) motivator, that clearly these two desires represent an
internal conflict (see Figure 5.6): the more control you have, the more
autonomy you sacrifice, and vice versa. Being in control restricts one's
independence of action because of the increased responsibility that it
entails!

Here, then, we come to the belief question: what is more important
for Daniel – to be in control or to be autonomous? As his Map indicated,

Daniel realised Spirit was now (keep in mind motivators change over time) more important to him than managing people; his discomfort at work had actually been this internal conflict. Part of him still longed for power and control; and another part of him wanted freedom and independence. This was manifesting in his business as indecision.[16] He knew now that he did not want to still be doing what he was currently doing in five years' time, yet he didn't know how to change or what in fact to change.

Daniel admitted he had actually been considering opening a new office in another area of the country, a move which would put considerable pressure on him personally and the business financially. But he felt compelled to take this action, though it felt uncomfortable and at odds with himself as to why.

We went deeper into his Map with him, whilst establishing his detailed personal history. We spotted that the Builder motivator at number 1 meant that he was really competitive and goal-oriented, but again there was another conflict in that he had Searcher at number 3, which was much more about collaboration in order to achieve purpose.

Builder (I want to be commercial) 28/40 versus Searcher (I want to make a difference) 24/40.

But being commercial means liking the tangible, the physical rewards, whereas making a difference more often focuses on values and the intangible (not always, however). Likely result? Internal conflict – two motivators pulling in two opposing directions. Not as severe as the Spirit and Director conflict, but now we have two internal oppositions in Daniel's top 4 motivators!!

Let's be clear about this: these motivational oppositions are exactly analogous to value conflicts; and when they are internal, as they are in Daniel's case, they represent that misalignment of our goals and our values at a deep level. It doesn't matter how capable Daniel is, what his advanced skill-set or knowledge-base is, if he feels divided internally, then he simply cannot function at the highest level. So, these internal conflicts have to be resolved.

As his Map is revealing so much, what does the coach need to prioritise? Here the PMA scores are really helpful, for these tell us how he is feeling about the realisation of his motivators in the work place (see Figure 5.7). Note, interestingly, even motivators that are not important – for example, in Daniel's case, the Friend – can be satisfied, and 9/10 means they are (though being not satisfied is also equally possible).

PMA SCORE		
Builder	9	indicates happy with financial rewards
Spirit	4	indicates chronic lack of discretionary time
Searcher	9	
Director	8	
Expert	9	
Star	9	
Creator	6	indicates too much routine/not a concern/ Link to Spirit issue
Defender	9	
Friend	9	

Figure 5.7 Highlighted PMA numbers for Daniel

If we look closely at this we see that Daniel does not go to work to belong socially, yet with 9/10 as his rating he is more than happy with his sense of friendship at work. What this tells us, as coaches, is that – PROBABLY[17] – he has good interpersonal skills, is friendly and staff like him. But as the Friend motivator is the lowest and he is satisfied, this is not an area of concern or one to work on. What is more striking is his second motivator: Spirit, 4/10. He desires autonomy but is chronically dissatisfied with his current state of independence, probably the discretionary use of his time, and his ability to prioritise his own actions. This is making him more than uncomfortable, especially if we take on board the point that we have already made: namely, that he is internally conflicted too!

Using these insights from his Map, Daniel realised that all his motivational efforts had been about avoidance, moving away from situations rather than towards what he truly wanted.

The classic example of why this is ineffective is in the example of people attempting to lose weight. Typically, in trying to lose weight the focus is always on losing what you don't want – avoidance in other words – so that when the weight is lost *and* the discomfort of being overweight disappears, so the motivation to continue evaporates, and the yo-yo principle kicks in and one is back to their old weight or worse! The avoidance motivation principle ('away from' pain in Freudian terms) has, as its underlying rationale, fear, and this always has a paralysing effect.

Motivational Maps, instead, considers what you really want ('moving towards' pleasure, in other, Freudian, terms). So, the implication is, the only way to effectively lose weight is to stop focusing on the weight and instead to focus on what you really want. What is that? Health, or attractiveness, or some other quality! There is some subtle analysis here which the coach can help the client unpick; what we are talking about is really one of the profoundest issues we face in human life: distinguishing between causes and symptoms, between the visible (what we seem to see) and the invisible[18] (what is below the surface but driving the real action). Too frequently managers are managing symptoms – a fire that never goes out – because, for whatever reason, they have no time to investigate causes. But this is not for the effective coach.

Case Study 5.3

Daniel's self-awareness

After discussion, Daniel understood this and realised too that his drive to succeed in business was largely driven by 'away from': away from poverty and some of the experiences he had had growing up in non-affluent circumstances. Knowing that, he could immediately see a pattern of boom and bust in his life where every time he had become comfortable he had metaphorically risked it all; he admitted that he did not want to go through that again. From this we set him the task of writing a new goal for what he actually wanted to achieve in his business and life, with the focus being on meaning more than materials, and on freedom and autonomy over control and power. This felt the right thing to do and was in alignment with his values in his Motivational Map.

At the next session Daniel had a new clarity: he wanted to reduce his work to four days a week; he categorically did not want to open up a new office (even though he strangely still felt compelled to do so). Further,

Daniel decided to hire a new Finance Director, so he could let go of a number of elements of his role that he had always done. And he also became aware of two more limiting beliefs which were part of the source of his inability to let go of control.

BELIEFS WHICH BLOCK DANIEL'S NATURAL CONFIDENCE
"I have 80 mouths to feed" and
"I have to be the first one in and the last one out of the office".[19]

Limiting beliefs are only limiting if they move the client away from their chosen goal. Daniel's new goals were now about personal freedom and progressing towards an abundant personal retirement; it was easy to see how those old beliefs, which had caused him to work very hard, were now no longer in alignment. It isn't easy to take an hour off, never mind a whole day, when you believe you have to be the first one in and last one out of the office!

The first step, then, is to break the power of the beliefs we subconsciously adopted when we were young. To become more aware of your own limiting beliefs do the following exercise.

ACTIVITY 5.8

Read to yourself your number 1 goal – your most important one – and ask: How do I *feel*?

How do I *feel* about it? (Not, what do I think about it?).

Now *dwell* on the answer to this question. Is there any discomfort? Are there any doubts? What thoughts come to mind? Pay attention to any sentences which may start like: *I can't, I'm not good enough, I don't deserve to, I'm not … , I need to be more …*

But if this still proves difficult, take one further step: imagine your life *as if* it were perfect. See yourself in: perfect health, the perfect weight and shape, with the perfect partner and family circumstances, in your dream role, with ample resources, and with the perfect work/life balance!

Can you imagine this? If so, ask what is it you believe about yourself which contradicts this perfect image? If not, slow down – take each component – health, weight, etc. – one step at a time.

Write down any limiting beliefs and thoughts about your Self that emerge as you go through this process. Also make a note of any inner conflicts that emerge, where part of you wants one outcome and another part of you wants a different, opposing outcome.

Finally, make a list of any negative memories from past events which you feel could be draining energy away from a desired outcome. Maybe you become aware that your drive to succeed is in part, like Daniel, largely driven by the need not to fail, which has emerged out of an emotional episode in childhood.

ACTIVITY 5.9

Create a bullet point list of Significant Emotional Events (see Figure 5.8) in your life and what emotion was present.

Are there links between the emotion and any patterns in your life? Daniel, for example, connected his early fear of poverty – I have not got enough – with being motivated only when he was at risk of losing it all. Hence the pattern of troughs and peaks in his business.

Limiting beliefs and negative emotions, then, are primary underpinning sources of the barriers, 'adversities', that obstruct our progress, but which present themselves as topics such as lack of Time or Money or as a People issues. So they are especially pernicious as they are invariably invisible. Their danger becomes particularly pronounced when our minds imagine futures in which our mistakes repeat themselves. The key next step, therefore, is to tease out what the beliefs are about these emotions and then re-frame then using the ABCDE method in Activities 5.4 and 5.5.

Summary

1   Time, money and people seem to be but are not the real barriers to success!
2   The true but invisible barriers are lack of confidence and belief.

Significant Emotional Events:	Emotions Present:
1	1
2	2
3	3
...	...

Figure 5.8 Significant emotional events

3   By developing awareness of your own specific barriers and obstacles to success you are well on the way to letting go of them.
4   We all have 24 hours in a day, so there is always enough time to achieve a truly congruent goal. What is likely to be missing is having our values aligned to our goal.
5   Using the Stop–Start Review can help us gain more control of our time and prioritise effectively.
6   Beliefs are only limiting if they move you away from what you truly desire.
7   The ABCDE method can help us reframe negative beliefs and enhance our performance.
8   Becoming aware of significant negative emotional events from the past shines light on the source of limiting beliefs and some of the patterns in our life.
9   Once you are aware of where your values, beliefs and motivators misalign to your goals, you can make a conscious choice to make changes where previously those choices didn't exist.

Notes

1   Cited in *The Time Paradox*, Philip Zimbardo, Rider Publishing (2008).
2   There are, of course, other barriers or blocks to success, and this book is really about just that: performance itself, and its three components we are discussing throughout, can be a block to success. Which means - lack of direction, lack of skills and knowledge training, and lack of motivation itself are all impediments to achieving what we want. But the principles of overcoming any barrier remain the same.
3   "The Self-Fulfilling Prophecy", Robert K. Merton, *Antioch Review*, 8.2 Summer (1948): "The self-fulfilling prophecy is, in the beginning, a false definition of the situation evoking a new behaviour which makes the original false conception come true". Merton, the originator of the phrase, clearly saw it in a negative light: 'a false definition', and equally clearly there are many negative applications of it. But another, more neutral, way of putting this is: "If men define situations as real, they are real in their consequences" - W.I. Thomas, *The Child in America* (1928). If we then create positive 'definitions' - or expectations - then we can expect positive consequences.
4   *Authentic Happiness*, Martin Seligman, Random House (2002): "Optimism and hope cause better resistance to depression when bad events strike, better performance at work, particularly in challenging jobs, and better physical health". Both optimism and hope are clearly 'belief' based.
5   The word confidence comes from the Latin, *con* = with and *fidence* = faith, so derives from the idea of being 'with faith'; clearly, faith and belief are synonymous, so what this comes down to is that weird and strange fact that beliefs at some root level determine all the outcomes of our lives.
6   Joseph M. Juran rediscovered the Pareto Principle, and coined the phrase 'the vital few', in his work on Quality in the 1950s: *Quality Control Handbook*, McGraw-Hill (1951).
7   It is important, of course, to understand that we should not attempt to make 100 per cent of our time wholly about engaging in the 'vital few'; that way madness lies. In any case it is impossible, as the 80/20 principle will also reassert itself, and we will find activities we considered 'vital' either prove not to be, or no longer are as things change.
8   *The Time Paradox*, Philip Zimbardo, Rider Publishing (2008). Zimbardo cites over 7 billion hits on Yahoo for 'time', with less than 3 billion for 'money' and less than 1 billion for 'sex'.

 9 Ellen Langer, *Counterclockwise: Mindful Health and the Power of Possibility,* Bal-
    lantine (2009).
10 The Placebo Effect can typically be 50-60 per cent effective; sometimes even higher:
    http://bit.ly/2taY4Mq.
11 Ford also said, germane to our topic: "There is no man living that cannot do more than
    he thinks he can". More at: http://bit.ly/2tmZ6QO.
12 The ABCDE model has gone through various adaptations from its origins with the
    psychologist Albert Ellis. Critically, it was taken up by Martin Seligman in his various
    works, including *Authentic Happiness*, ibid.
13 As Martin Seligman observes in *Authentic Happiness*: "It is essential to realise that
    your beliefs are just that - beliefs. They may or may not be facts", ibid.
14 In Chapter 8 we deal with the topic of values, another word that might be appropriate
    here. Values really are beliefs that we attach a special emotional significance to. And
    the motivators themselves, given their emotional nature, partially generate values, or
    beliefs that we are attached to. So, for example, a strong Searcher motivator might
    indicate a value like 'serving the customer is important' or a belief such as 'having a
    strong sense of purpose'.
15 So, the goal is to be financially independent, but how will that play out when money
    does not motivate and our (probably inherited) belief is that money is difficult to make?
    The coach works on the belief directly, and the motivator indirectly. Indirectly means,
    rather than trying to change the motivator, we ask the question: If I don't want to
    make money intensely, what practical steps, systems, processes, protocols do I need to
    implement, so that I can still achieve my goal?
16 Motivational Maps is a non-stereotyping tool and this should be obvious because moti-
    vations change over time. That said, we frequently find certain occupations, roles and
    positions which do have 'typical' profiles. One of the them is the owner Managing
    Directors of SMEs in the UK. Frequently, we find that the combination of the Direc-
    tor and Spirit motivator in the top three of their profile is an unexamined source of
    problem to them. Entrepreneurs tend to be 'independent' Spirit mavericks who like
    controlling people and resources, and the internal tension of these two motivators can
    lead to powerful and detrimental effects.
17 PROBABLY - is a key word in interpreting Maps; nothing means any one thing defini-
    tively; one must always consider context; and always never force an interpretation on
    the client. That said, the Maps do have an amazing predictive ability.
18 Clearly, this is a point very germane to Chapter 3 and the discussion we had on the
    Pareto Principle and the 20 per cent - the vital few - that are often overlooked.
19 See Chapter 4 for a fuller list of disempowering beliefs in seven important categories,
    and also a complementary set of empowering beliefs to remedy them.

6 Unblocking one more barrier to success: People

We have been looking throughout this book at self-sabotaging blocks to our performance and success, including the excuse of time and money as negative factors. We saw how this was usually related to our subconscious priorities and beliefs; also, if you have completed your Motivational Map, how motivators can help us understand currently how we prioritise time in relation to our work or business. We also gave you some exercises to help you begin to consider thinking differently about those priorities to assist you towards your new goal.

We now need to consider the issue of other PEOPLE blocking us! Before tackling this from a mapping and coaching perspective, it may be as well to consider all the reasons why we have difficulties with other people.

ACTIVITY 6.1

Conflicts with other people

List all the reasons why you think we frequently find ourselves in conflict with others. What do you consider to be the top three reasons? What ideas do you have to mitigate or resolve these kinds of conflicts?

We can think of at least nine reasons why conflicts occur, and they are listed in Figure 6.1.

We cannot deal with all these causes in this chapter, but a couple of points do need noting. First, what we mean by 'validity'. What we mean by this is whether the reason is actually legitimate. For example, is having different aims, objectives or goals to another person right or normal? Yes, it is; it's part of life: you want to run in a marathon but Fred wants to play poker. The goals are different but equally valid. And so too with all the other categories, up to and including motivators: we note especially that it is OK[1] to have conflicting motivators, this is normal!

The 9 Reasons	Problem	Validity	Likely Response
GOALS	Differences	Yes	Clarification
VALUES	Clashing	Yes	Understanding/Empathy
RESOURCES	Scarce	Yes	Negotiation
PERSONALITIES	Opposing	Yes	Understanding/Modelling
MOTIVATIONS	Conflicting	Yes	Understanding/Modelling
IGNORANCE	Deliberate OR unintentional	Either	Explanation
EGO	Self-importance	No	Assertiveness
GAME PLAYING	Deficiency needs	No	Boundaries
PATHOLOGY	I'm NOT OK, You're NOT OK	No	Avoidance

Figure 6.1 Reasons for conflict

But when we come to ignorance, it is perhaps normal to be unintentionally igno-rant about some topic or issue, since we all are from time to time. It is less valid, perhaps, to be and to remain deliberately ignorant. And so we progress – or regress – to the last three conflict issues which we claim are not valid: ego, game playing, and pathology. These 'states' or conditions of mind all represent a situation wherein the individual acts in a non-rational way, frequently blocking their own ability to achieve their true goals or desires. All three states reveal low, even chronically low, self-esteem, which means that there is invariably a follow-through issue even if the coach can get the client to accept and understand their condition. So, whilst a coach may encounter such people, their treatment is more aligned with therapy or counselling rather than coaching properly deployed, although the coach may well be able to help.

But in answer to the question, what do you consider to be the top three reasons for conflict, then the answer is almost certainly going to be: value clashes, goal dif-ferences and what is called personality problems. And it is on this last point – the number of people who say that there is a 'personality clash' at work, or even within the family – that we want to resume our coaching theme. For, oftentimes, what is perceived to be a personality clash can in reality be a motivational clash; indeed, we think that 'personality clash' is frequently a lazy shorthand for those not both-ering to look beneath the surface – where the energies are in a constant ferment.

So, to return to our focus, remember what we said in Chapter 2 that PERCEP-TION IS PROJECTION!

Do we see here two faces facing each other or a candlestick? Similarly, in physics, is it a wave of light or a particle? It all depends on how we choose to observe it. We project[2] onto other people exactly what we want to see, and often this involves some aspect of our own personality, issues, or 'shadow-side'.

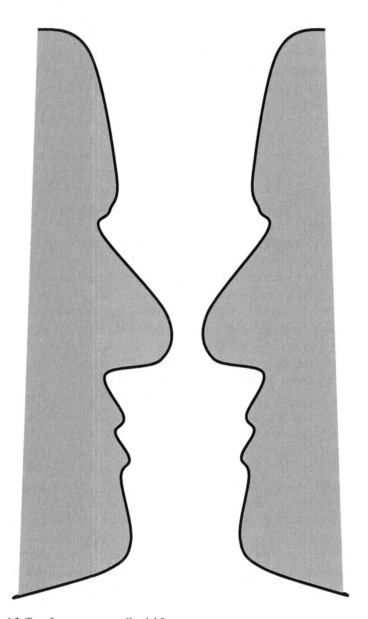

Figure 6.2 Two faces or one candlestick?

Case Study 6.1

Mary the golfer

Mary is a female golfer with lots of potential and ability and who also derived a lot of enjoyment from the game. A game she had temporarily given up! At the first coaching session she explained the bullying experienced at her latest golf club. As we explored this issue more deeply, it was no surprise for either of us to find previous bullying incidents experienced at university, in an early relationship, a previous job and also previously within golf. At one point within the session she stated quite vociferously, "I hate people negatively judging others".

The particular incident which had caused her to leave the club involved her being negatively judged by a particular female member of the golf club for something which had happened by accident on the golf course. Mary was asked how she felt when she thought of that individual? She was then asked what she thought of her own judgements on this particular lady?

It was a key moment for Mary to realise that she herself was negatively judging this lady for negatively judging her, which was precisely the thing she said she hated. In short, she realised she had become the enemy she was fighting! Once we do this we become divided internally; we are fighting in the external world the judgements and values which we ourselves have embraced. And, as one religious text put it: a house divided cannot stand.

The starting point, then, for countering this tendency is to take a holistic approach: before we influence the other person, we have to be able to influence ourselves. In dealing with other people 'blocking' us, we need to unblock ourselves first. This is not easy but both the psychological literature and the spiritual traditions all point to the same solution: forgiveness. We have to forgive others or else we become trapped in a cycle of negative emotions often worse than the provocations we have experienced. Furthermore, not to forgive means the wrong done to us lives on in our psyches because we go on feeding it with our bitterness and resentments. To be clear, therefore, we are not saying that forgiveness is comfortable; revenge comes much more easily to our ego. And we are not saying forgiveness means some sort of happy-clappy, 'so that's all right then', and we act as if the wrong done us has never happened. That would be naïve; we forgive but we may not forget; and the not forgetting means we can act prudently in our future interactions, or lack of them, with that person. So, to take the example of Mary at the golf club, she can forgive the woman, but it may be in future that she doesn't seek out her company, albeit remaining unaffected when in it.

Thus, this forgiveness needs not only to be for people whom we perceive may have wronged us in the past, but also for ourselves and our negative judgements we have made about ourselves over the years. We need to forgive ourselves. This is important to stop the inner corrosion that builds up – sort of emotional toxins – from guilt we experience over time. Forgiveness – a letting-go of the anger, resentment and bitterness – we feel towards other people who have wronged us is like a rush of powerful, fresh, clean water clearing out an old, blocked, furred up pipe or tube. It opens up more possibilities for us; it revitalises us. In fact, the best description of forgiveness possibly is of it being completely giving forth of oneself without holding back. If we are able to forgive completely then, in the future, we are able to completely give forth of our self, and in all future relationships benefit arises.

ACTIVITY 6.2

Practising Tonglen

The Buddhists have a practice called Tonglen, which is a way of increasing compassion for other people. It is a simple process, which if it can become a habit, changes how we typically think of and feel about others. Try the following in a quiet space:

1   Close your eyes and focus on your breath
2   Breathing through the nose (where possible) aim to slowly increase the exhalation; increasing the length of the exhalation relaxes you
3   Breathe out good feelings and warmth towards the difficult person who offends you
4   Breathe in their suffering and pain – imagine how they feel – empathise with them
5   Repeat the process several times and note how you feel

Perhaps it helps us to be more compassionate if we remember Philo of Alexandria's reported view: 'Be kind. Everyone you meet is carrying a big problem'[3]. People who strike out at you have their problems too.

If that isn't enough here are two reasons more why is it so important to forgive and clear the negative images we have up of others:

1: It helps us to heal – emotionally and spiritually (which can lead to physical and mental healing) and become more whole and complete. Our lives can then enjoy greater levels of peace and contentment.

2: It drastically improves your ability to perceive people in a positive light and hence be able to positively influence them (remember perception is projection). To increase your influence over others is tantamount to increasing your power. Think about it: when you totally and utterly reject somebody and refuse to forgive them, then they tend to erect massive barriers towards you and your interests and positions.

Two real examples illustrate points 1 and 2.

Case study 6.2

Paula and Hitler

Paula attended a Master Practitioner NLP Course. Previously she found it difficult to fully let go of her negative emotion and judgements of other people, especially around cruelty. At one poignant moment, with her eyes shut tight, she asked the trainer, "So you would ask me to forgive Hitler?". Surprisingly, the trainer replied, "Yes, otherwise it is you that is drinking poison and expecting someone else to suffer".

This example reveals several things:

a) The egoic mind trying to cling onto its sense of identity. An identity that has to be right by virtue of another being wrong;

b) the need for all of us to be able to forgive – to let go – if we are to heal effectively; this is not done for anyone else's benefit (although others, especially our loved ones, do benefit), it is for our enabling personal journey to continue, and not to be stuck in the negativity of the past. Victor Frankl put it this way: "The last of human freedoms is the ability to choose one's attitude in a given set of circumstances." [4]

Case Study 6.3

Bevis and Jim

As a young Leisure Centre Manager Bevis truly loved his job. Given freedom to manage in his own way, he had no problems but one: Jim. Struggling to get his point across in senior management meetings, he found Jim kept blocking his contributions. Jim had worked for the organisation almost straight out of university and had worked his way up to Leisure Centre Manager at a different site to Bevis, and he provided stern resistance to Bevis's ideas. Bevis saw Jim himself as the problem.

Fast forward a decade and now Jim and Bevis are good friends; Jim is someone Bevis can count on. Indeed, Bevis sees him as one of the most genuine, caring and loyal people he knows. Furthermore, he is someone who has used Bevis's business services (having left the Leisure Centre) on a number of occasions to help develop his team.

What changed? Here is where the explanatory power of the Motivational Maps shows what was going on, and how through it greater awareness, communication, rapport and team-working improved.

If we look at the top 3 motivators of Jim and Bevis we find the following:

Jim's 3	DEFENDER	EXPERT	SEARCHER
Wants	*security*	*learning*	*making a difference*
Bevis's 3	SPIRIT	SEARCHER	CREATOR
Wants	*independence*	*making a difference*	*innovation*

ACTIVITY 6.3

A comparison of Jim and Bevis's Maps

If we look at these three top motivators and realise that these are 'wants' or underlying energies that drive their behaviours, usually subconsciously, then what do we see?

Make some notes on what this might mean for their relationship. Take note that they share 'one' motivator in their respective top three, but that each has two other motivators. What does the one in common suggest? And what do the others indicate? Give this some serious thought before studying our response.

At this point we are keeping it simple, just considering the top three, most important motivators as they apply to Jim and Bevis.

Jim's Defender means he wants to have security, stability, predictability and routine; the question here to ask yourself is: does someone wanting security like risk or change? Of course not!

By way of contrast, Bevis wants freedom, autonomy of decision making, independence and hates micro management; the question here is the same, does someone wanting freedom like risk or change? Of course!

Hence, we have right up front a fundamental conflict. But the conflict is not just that they have different motivators, which is somewhat obvious. No, it goes down into a deeper, more invisible and subtle level of their psyche: how risk and change appear to them both. One thrives on it; the other rejects it. Neither position is good or bad, but context determines everything. So if we put a negative spin on both their attitudes it would be that Bevis's embrace of risk and change may be or may become reckless, and so destructive; and Jim's avoidance of risk and change may be or may become timidity, and so conformist.

Alternatively, if we put a positive spin on their respective attitudes, Bevis is bold and adventurous, whereas Jim's position is analytical and planned.

Alternating between these two poles of a positive AND negative spin on what the Map might mean without committing prematurely to either is a central concept in advanced coaching practice for Motivational Maps; too many jump too readily to one interpretation or the other.

Ideally, it is the senior person, the manager, who will take responsibility for accommodating or matching the motivators of their subordinates. However, in Bevis's own words:

> *"Once I became aware of Jim's Defender motivator, and its strengths and weaknesses, everything changed. I went from seeing Jim as a block to my changes, and instead realised that his main focus was on protecting his team and keeping things stable and secure for them.*
>
> *Thus, it was my way of communicating change that was the issue; I needed to take ownership of it. Understanding his DEFENDER motivation, I was able to consistently improve my level of influence both with Jim and other, even more senior members of the management structure. Each and every time I spoke about the potential for change I first considered the impact on team members and re-framed the benefits of my ideas based upon how they would improve long term security and stability for the team."*

This became crucial in effecting real and significant changes to the Leisure Centre.

Case Study 6.4

Trust status

The Leisure Centre considered moving to Trust status. Should they go for it? Note the alternative language used in this example.

Bevis's Language and Pitch BEFORE Map Awareness:

> A. *"Taking the Leisure Centre to Trust status will benefit us, as it will empower us to create a new Culture, to be able to innovate and find new more efficient ways of doing things; this will lead not only to better results but a more meaningful way of doing business!"*

Bevis's Language and Pitch AFTER Map Awareness (specifically considering the dominance of Defender motivator in Jim and other senior staff profiles):

> B. *"Taking the Leisure Centre to Trust status will benefit us, as it will empower us to be fully in charge of our own decision making, meaning we can protect our staff and eliminate the risk of decisions being made above our heads, which negatively impact our performance and hence the future security of the service."*

ACTIVITY 6.4

a   Compare sentence A. with Bevis's top three motivators. Which words reflect some aspects of his top 3 motivators?

b   Compare sentence B. with Jim's top three motivators. Which words reflect some aspects of his top 3 motivators?[5]

c   Remember: Bevis can choose to speak either sentence A. or B. Given that Jim is his boss (and others like Jim) which sentence is most likely to influence Jim?[6]

With this in mind, then, what if other motivators were in Jim's top three (or Bevis's for that matter – and keep in mind everyone's motivators change over time)? Let's take a moment to look at the nine motivational drivers again (see Figure 6.3).

ACTIVITY 6.5

a)   Take a look at these nine motivators and their simple three word or phrase definitions. Ask yourself these two questions:

    o   Which motivators seem to complement each other?
    o   Which motivators seem to clash with each other?

We have considered the conflict between Jim's Defender and Bevis's Spirit. But consider this: what if one and the same person had Defender and Spirit within their own profile as first and second motivators, equally or very closely scored? What would that mean or do?[7]

One should note on this chart (see Figure 6.4) that some tensions or internal incompatibilities are not always the case; most notably the Expert with the Creator. These can be a wonderfully complementary pairing within the psyche of an individual, as learning feeds creativity and vice versa; but sometimes – if one reflects on what one sees – an individual may have deep learning which is 'frozen', as it were, and they become rigid in their application of knowledge. In short, non-creative. This is another example of alternating between two poles of positive and negative interpretation without that irritable reaching after facts prematurely!

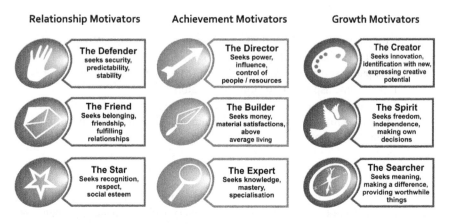

Figure 6.3 Model of the nine motivators

Motivator	Tensions in order of intensity		
Searcher	Defender	Builder	
Spirit	Director	Defender	Friend
Creator	Defender	Director	Expert
Expert	Creator		
Builder	Friend	Searcher	
Director	Spirit	Friend	Creator
Star	Searcher	Spirit	
Friend	Spirit	Director	Builder
Defender	Searcher	Creator	Spirit

Figure 6.4 Internal individual motivational compatibility chart

ACTIVITY 6.6

Reviewing your Map for potential conflict with others

a) Take a look at your lowest Map motivator(s). Take a moment to understand more about your lowest motivator. Specifically note any motivators scoring less than 10.
b) Is there someone you find difficult AND whose behaviours (or Map scores if you know them!) demonstrate an alignment with your lowest motivational preference(s)?
c) How might better understanding their motivational preference, which may be your lowest, improve your interaction with that person?
d) How does understanding that motivational preference help you see, or reframe, that person (remember there are no wrong motivators)?

MOTIVATORS	TENSIONS
DEFENDER v. SEARCHER	tension between conservation and improvement
DEFENDER v. CREATOR	tension between stability and innovation
DEFENDER v. SPIRIT	tension between security and freedom
DIRECTOR v. SPIRIT	control and autonomy
DIRECTOR v. FRIEND	tension between managing and friendship
BUILDER v. SEARCHER	tension between materialism and idealism

Figure 6.5 The most common potential Motivational Map conflicts

Understanding Map preferences, then, can help us better communicate with 'difficult' others (see Figure 6.5).

These 'potential' conflicts first occur within our own profiles; we find ourselves drawn in two opposing directions. But equally we can experience what we call 'polarity reinforcement' whereby motivators are at opposite ends of the profile, and so reinforce the strong motivator at the top end.

To give an example of this, let's take the 'tension', which is very common in certain sectors[8] of Searcher top motivator and Defender in second place. This is not good or bad in itself, but clearly the individual is being pulled in two contrary directions; this may have benefits or not. But now imagine the situation whereby somebody has Searcher No. 1 and Defender No. 9, which is the lowest motivator (and of course, equally, imagine Defender No. 1 and Searcher No. 9). This is where we get polarity reinforcement: if Defender is 9th, then its power to minimise improvements and change is lessened, so that the energy to drive improvements – the making a difference of the Searcher – is thereby heightened. It is important to realise of course that more than just two motivators may be involved in this polarity reinforcement; we see from the examples that we could have a situation where Defender is No.1 AND Creator and Searcher are No. 8 and No. 9 in the order, so that both their energies for change do not dilute the energy of conservation and stability that the Defender wants.

Where these polarity reinforcements occur, therefore, especially in our own profiles, we are going to find it difficult[9] communicating with someone who has a reverse polarity reinforcement to ourselves! So imagine you are (see Figure 6.6):

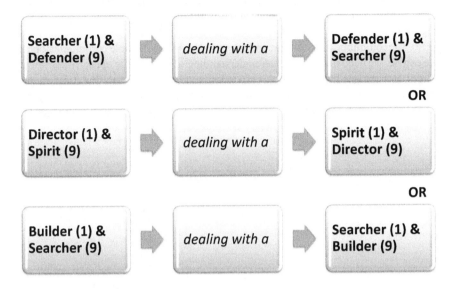

Figure 6.6 Polarity reinforcements

ACTIVITY 6.7

- Check to see if you have any polarity reinforcement in your nine motivators. Reflect on whether, therefore (and we need to be clear that there is nothing wrong with not experiencing this 'strength', it may depend on the intensity of the scoring), you are aware of how particularly strong your top motivator feels to be.
- Consider the lowest motivator in your polarity reinforcement. This is what you don't want, and it's made more palpable as what you do want is stronger. But what is it, exactly, that you don't desire? What exactly turns you off? Write it down.
- Now review the three people you find the most difficult to deal with (this can be at work or personal). Analyse why you find them difficult. Go beyond behavioural characteristics (e.g. they are rude) to trying to identify the underlying motivational disposition. You do this by asking the question: When I look at their words and behaviour I notice that what they really want is ... What's the answer? Power (so, Director motivator), Recognition (so, Star motivator), Friendship (so, Friend motivator) and so on through the other six types.
- Finally, notice whether sometimes the motivator driving their behaviour is your lowest in the polarity reinforcement we have described.

The chance of conflict and misunderstanding, then, is heightened when we have contrasting profiles with other people. How might this play out in practice? See Figure 6.7.

So, for communication to flow, and for us to become as flexible communicators as we can be, we need to gain a greater understanding of the benefits of each of the motivators; like attracts like and people respond more to the motivators that drive *them*.

One further incentive to adopt this way of thinking about others is this: in any situation we find ourselves in regarding difficult people, we have a choice. Do we want to be right, or do we want to be effective? To be right means that we

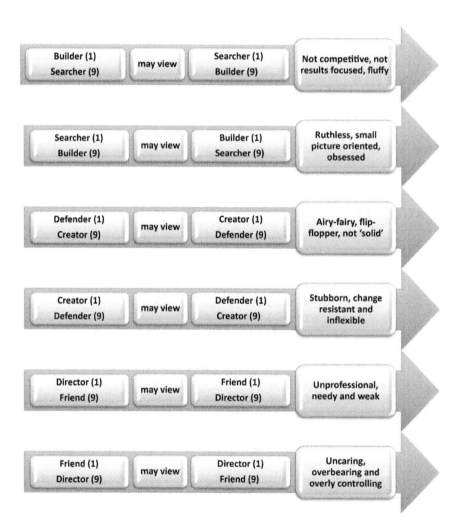

Figure 6.7 Polarity reinforcement contrasts

are going to prove that somebody else is wrong; this is always disputatious, and leads to people sticking their heels in, even when they know they are wrong. They mustn't lose face. On the other hand, to be effective means: to get a good result, often for yourself, but even better for you and the other person. This is typically called a win–win situation.

Thus, being effective is not about being 'right'; it is about understanding, first and foremost, where the other person is coming from. Usually this only means their intellectual position, but in using the Maps we are also suggesting that we include where they are coming from motivationally, energetically, emotionally. This way we have far more chance of success.

We have seen from Bevis's approach to Jim how his language changed when he realised how different their motivational profiles were; and how Bevis needed to incorporate far more 'Defender-speak' into his propositions in order to get them accepted – which they were more frequently. But there is also another important Map principle here that applies both to your own personal development and to how we deal with other, especially difficult, people – and unblock the barriers.

It should be evident by now that motivation is like health and fitness; in other words, motivation is something we need to maintain on an ongoing and regular basis. Once we have done our Map, then we have a firm basis on which we can plan or plot our motivational inputs over the succeeding 18 months or so. Before we do that, however:

ACTIVITY 6.8

Think about your own personal development. What do you do to ensure that your motivational levels remain high? How does this relate to your own Motivational Map? What suggestions from your Map have you taken on board? What suggestions might you in future consider doing?

When we target specific rewards for our self, we call this Reward Strategies. Whether we are doing this consciously or not, it is what, if you will, keeps us going, keeps us motivated. And we need to be motivated for we already know that there is a powerful correlation between performance and high levels of motivation. But there is also another significant connection: between motivation and attractiveness. We become more attractive (generally speaking, and accepting that profoundly negative people[10] tend to resent others who shine via their energy, as they lack it) to other people when we are high energy. The stars of screen, film, TV, sport and even politics that we most like and enjoy are invariably (whatever they may actually be off-screen or out of the public eye) high energy individuals.

So, to become more attractive as people – which increases our influence – we need to become more motivated; as coaches too we are leaders, and clients take their cue from the energy level of the coach. This, then, is another reason for high energy levels in every encounter. What do we need to do to reward ourselves?

The key thing to grasp is a. we need to reward ourselves often and frequently, so that it forms a habit, and b. the rewards can be small, micro-rewards, and c. that we have usually three top motivators to replenish. From your Map you will know your satisfaction rating – or PMA – score with these three top motivators, so you can identify which ones especially need 'feeding'. See Figure 6.8.

ACTIVITY 6.9

Review Figure 6.8. Given your motivational profile, what small things – micro-rewards – might you give yourself in the near future? Link the rewards to achievements or progress along the way to meeting your goals or targets. Form a habit of topping up your motivators.

	REWARD #1	REWARD #2	REWARD #3	BIG REWARD
SEARCHER	Ask for quality feedback	Improve your environment in a small way	Ensure fit for purpose equipment	Align your work with your values
SPIRIT	Dress down where you can	Allocate 10 per cent of time to *your* project	Remove red tape; outsource something	Create a 5 year vision of where you want to be
CREATOR	Avoid routines	Set goal needing creative solution	Find course on being creative	Take sabbatical for something different

Figure 6.8a, b and c Three micro-reward strategies for the coach + one big reward

	REWARD #1	REWARD #2	REWARD #3	BIG REWARD
EXPERT	Buy book on *expert* topic	Volunteer to run volunteer training	Ask each evening, Was I better at …?	Develop serious new level of mastery
BUILDER	Review career options	Give yourself small perks for achieving targets	Enter a sport or social competition	Re-set financial goals
DIRECTOR	Find a mentor	Log daily 3 achievements in journal	Stretch yourself – go outside your comfort zone	Commit to major leadership programme

	REWARD #1	REWARD #2	REWARD #3	BIG REWARD
STAR	Buy quality clothes & accessories	Ensure a conspicuous business card	Find a prominent role model and imitate	Ensure you have *letters* after your name that you may deploy
FRIEND	Ring a friend	Listen intently	Contribute to the team in a small way	Consider your top 5 relationships and how you will deepen them over time
DEFENDER	Plan your week	Allocate time for administrative tasks	Reduce clutter	Review your long-term goals

Figure 6.8 (Continued)

	HOT BUTTONS	OPPORTUNITIES FOR CLIENT
Searcher	Meaning & Make a Difference	Creating mission statement
Spirit	Freedom & Independence	Generating 5 year vision
Creator	Innovation & Change	Creatively solving 'Big Problem'
Expert	Expertise & Mastery	Becoming one of top 4 per cent of experts in their field
Builder	Money & Material Satisfaction	Surpassing financial goals
Director	Power & Influence	Assuming more responsibility or gaining promotion
Star	Recognition & Respect	Achieving public recognition of achievements
Friend	Belonging & Friendship	Being highly valued as core team member
Defender	Security & Predictability	Ensuring all processes, especially communications, are systemised

Figure 6.9 Big opportunities for clients

Now we come to sustaining or improving the motivation of the client. Again, there will be big picture motivators that are immediately evident (see Figure 6.9).

These are all big picture things the client wants; but the coach can quickly establish whether they have them or to what degree they have them; and then help them re-commit to their achievement. If we just take the first one, The Searcher, then mission or purpose is central to their well-being; they want to engage in meaningful activities that contribute to their life's purpose. But for all that, in our experience, we find time and time again, including when we coach coaches, that so many people have not created a Mission Statement[11] which they can refer to as their compass as they move forward.

What, then, about those micro-rewards that we can suggest to the client that can help keep them motivated on a daily or weekly or monthly basis? See Figure 6.10.

These ideas – and of course they are not exhaustive – are there to help us motivate our clients more, so they, like us, become high energy individuals. In this way a number of benefits accrue: we are more attractive as high energy people, more influential, and actually more resilient. Being highly motivated provides an increase in wellbeing as well as energy, and we find we can cope with more, including handling the difficult people who set up barriers to what we want to

	REWARD #1	REWARD #2	REWARD #3	BIG REWARD
SEARCHER	Ask 3 customers for feedback	Identify the most important *verb* that characterises them	Upgrade their personal computer system	Align your work with your values
SPIRIT	Do the Stop–Start review	Help them identify their no. 1 priority	Take one step to make work environment more relaxing	Create a 5 year vision of where you want to be
CREATOR	Get them brainstorming about processes	Ask them how they would reward themselves when they *are* creative?	Get them to create their own motivational poster	Take sabbatical for something different

	REWARD #1	REWARD #2	REWARD #3	BIG REWARD
EXPERT	Ask them to 'explain' their area of expertise to you – and listen	Get them to book on one training course in next 6 months	Suggest they nominate one book a month that improves performance	Develop serious new level of mastery
BUILDER	Top up supply of chocolate/cake/ tea or coffee	Allow them to have pocket money for *them*	Review papers/internet for new opportunities	Re-set financial goals
DIRECTOR	Devise a clear career development path	Undertake a 360 Review of Strengths and Weaknesses	Buy a book on delegation skills	Commit to major leadership programme

Figure 6.10a, b and c Three micro-reward strategies for the client

	REWARD #1	REWARD #2	REWARD #3	BIG REWARD
STAR	Update CV	Create a private space where any badges, cups, trophies, certificates can be displayed	Inform others of what they have achieved: messages, newsletters, press, social media	Ensure you have *letters* after your name that you may deploy
FRIEND	Suggest they praise/feedback to a colleague	Create a plan to deal with someone they find difficult	Insist their team has a social dimension	Consider your top 5 relationships and how you will deepen them over time
DEFENDER	Review the forthcoming week/month	Check their current investments/ pension arrangements	Put in writing what they are going to achieve in the year	Review your long-term goals

Figure 6.10 (Continued)

achieve. And we can do this by micro-rewards to ourselves; and secondly, we reward others, subtly, in the same way, thus creating a positive and upward spiral of energy.

We have come a long way in this chapter, and yet can scarcely claim to have covered the fullness of a topic such as unblocking the people barrier, but a couple of things should be clear. First, we have emphasised the importance of unblocking oneself – and the power of forgiveness – in the first instance. Secondly, we have roundly promoted the counterintuitive idea that motivation can make a massive difference to the way we interact with others, and that many barriers can be removed if we use the principles (if not the actual Maps themselves) of Motivational Mapping.

There is one final thing to say on this, and that is this. Self-development follows a well-trodden path, which, like the Maps themselves, are counterintuitive. They are counterintuitive in that most people practise self-development backwards. It goes something like this: 'If I had 10 million pounds or dollars, THEN I could do whatever I want, and THEN I'd be really happy'. Notice the sequence: HAVE–DO–BE. This is all wrong for many reasons, and almost never ends happily. Our self-esteem has a way of recalibrating the balance. We see this most prominently with big lottery[12] winners. It is estimated that over 30 per cent or more of the big winners end up eventually 'losing' the fortunes they won by chance: in their *being* they did not feel worth the fortune, and as they had done nothing meaningful to acquire it, so their subconscious minds – and its limiting beliefs – has taken over and allowed them to fritter it all away.

The correct personal development sequence, then, is BEING first, then DOING, and when they are aligned we have HAVING (or GETTING). So we need to generate:

'To be' goals
'To do' goals
'To have' goals

And in that order really. We start with personal development – to be/to become – rather than what we want to achieve or have. This is especially, and critically, true of all leaders, and we will be saying a lot more about this in the forthcoming companion volume to this called *Mapping Motivation for Leadership*.[13]

And therefore in order to have what we want, we need to do what we need to do, and for us to be able to do that from a position of power, we need to be the kind of person, firstly, from whom that kind of doing flows! We need to be congruent – be, do, and have are aligned. There is of course a feedback loop here that is summed up in the phrase 'fake it till you make it'. This expresses the idea that by committing to certain actions and habits we can become the kind of people we want to be; in other words, by persistently doing things we can and will affect who we are[14] – going up a level – and also by doing so may well acquire – have (going down a level) – 'things' as well. Hence, our actions – our doings – sit at a central see-saw point in our development.

We think this ties in with Maslow's Hierarchy of Needs in that people can advance up the Hierarchy, and move towards self-actualisation, but also can descend back down as a response to urgencies, emergencies and situations that change their fundamental perceptions of themselves and their reality. And so, if that is true of Maslow, then it is true of the Maps. As we like to say: motivations change over time. No state is intrinsically 'superior', although 'being' is the preferred and ultimate state we desire if only because the others – doing/having – are endless; that is to say, we often find we cannot exhaust our desire to acquire 'stuff' (think shopaholics!) or stop ourselves doing 'things' (think workaholics!). But 'being' is entire and complete of itself; therefore, being is a state of peace, and thus peace of mind, and so our ultimate desire. We rest content with our self; it is in fact our still point in the turning world, and if we are centred there, all things are possible. Lao Tzu expressed it this way: "To the mind that is still, the whole universe surrenders."[15]

If we consider the three elements (RAG) of Maps, then we do encounter a parallel world (see Figure 6.11 on the next page).

Various elements of Mapping are now drawn together: the three primary divisions of motivators into Relationship, Achievement and Growth, their links to Feel–Think–Know modes of communicating, Past–Present–Future orientation, the self-concept's tripartite division into self-esteem, self-image and ideal self,[16]

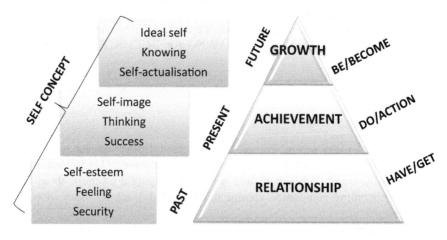

Figure 6.11 Have, Do, Be and the RAG triangle

and three respective foci: how our sense of security is inseparably bound to our Relationships – we HAVE relationships; our sense of success is inseparably bound to our Achievement – we DO achievements; and our sense of self-actualisation inseparably bound to our Growth – we BECOME who we are[17]! Note the word PRESENT next to the Achievement cluster in Figure 6.11: in this we refer to taking action in the present, as opposed to living presently in the moment, which is independent of the motivational preferences. It is independent because 'living presently in the moment' is a spiritual – in the widest sense of the word – practice, which all three elements of motivation, R, A, and G, can access if they choose.

Of course, as children the Maslow hierarchy goes from Have to Do to Be. We have relationships with our parents that provide the necessary security to enable us to Do things – like walk for the first time, or like leaving home eventually – and then as adults we become fully who we are. But this assumes we have had that security, that we have had those early successes which we did, to give us the confidence to become who we really are, and that BE–DO–HAVE is our norm. However, this is a big assumption, and it is why the process can reverse under stress (back to HAVE–DO–BE) as adults try to feel better by doing and having more in a never ending failed cycle: most people do not feel enough security, and did not achieve at the level they wanted growing up[18], and often spend time trying to prove something in adult life to overcome what they felt they lacked earlier in life. This is why the focus has to switch to BEING, and personal development as the priority – necessitating DOING and HAVING following in its wake.

In this way, then, we come full circle to dealing with the most difficult block of all in dealing with others: our Self.

ACTIVITY 6.10

Ask yourself these questions.

1   What has your focus in life over the last three years been mostly about:

having or acquiring relationships, or
doing or achieving things, or
being or becoming who you are?

2   What does your Map RAG score tell you? Does it align with your having-doing-being choices or does it seem at variance? For example, you focus on personal development (BE) but your Map profile is dominantly Relationship-driven (R)? Or, you focus on acquiring material possessions (DO) but your Map profile is dominantly Growth (G).

3   Reflect on these issues. What feelings, thoughts, actions emerge for you regarding your next steps?

4   Finally, how do these issues help you consider unblocking the people barriers in your life?

Summary

1   There are nine major reasons why we find ourselves in conflict with others.
2   Personality conflicts are often motivational conflicts.
3   Practising forgiveness on a regular basis is good for others and good for us psychologically.
4   Contrasting motivations can lead to serious blockages in dealing with others.
5   Adapting one's language to match another's motivational preferences can be highly effective.
6   Understanding where motivators conflict and where there is 'polarity reinforcement' is important.
7   'Polarity reinforcements' can easily exaggerate unwitting stereotyping of other people.
8   Practising Reward and Micro-reward strategies on ourselves and our clients can have profoundly motivating effects.
9   Self-development follows the Being–Doing–Having sequence, not the other way around.

Notes

1   The I'm NOT OK, You're NOT OK is the pathological condition identified in Transactional Analysis as "Lose-Lose". Thomas Harris writes: "There is a kind of miserable

sense in this, in that the integrity of the position is maintained, but it leads to despair. The ultimate resolution of this position is giving up (leading to institutionalisation) or suicide". From *I'm OK, You're OK*, Pan (1973).

2 Projection is one of the 'big' three psychological problems - or Defence Mechanisms - that beset all people, even those in relatively good psychological health. If left unattended, or uncorrected, they produce serious mental problems and breakdowns. The two other 'big' problems are Denial and Blame. The beginning of 'correcting' the problem starts with self-awareness of it; without the self-awareness we do not even recognise the problem. In calling these the 'big' three, this is not to minimise the severity of other issues such as: Repression, Identification, Substitution, Reaction Formation, Rationalisation, Sublimation and so on.

3 Cited in James Hollis, *Finding Meaning in the Second Half of Life*, Gotham Books (2006).

4 Our example may seem extreme, but it is the essence of what Victor Frankl's book demonstrates more clearly than any other: the need to be able to forgive even in the most extreme of circumstances: *Man's Search for Meaning*, Hodder and Stoughton (1946).

5 Clear examples would be 'empower': Spirit; 'create', 'new', 'innovate': Creator; 'more efficient', 'meaningful': Searcher. Note that since Jim shares the Searcher motivator, they may have some influence on him. Clear examples of words from Jim's motivational profile would be: 'fully in charge', 'protect our staff', 'eliminate the risk', 'future security'. Note here, too, that Bevis does not even use language that might trigger approval from Jim's second and third motivators: satisfying the critical first one is enough (in this case).

6 Sentence B of course.

7 The motivators can be exactly and equally scored; however, the programme has an 8-level algorithm built into it, which means that it can still decide what ultimately the correct ranking is even when the scores are drawn.

8 In a data review of 432 maps in Accountancy, 708 in Financial Services, 657 in Hospital Healthcare, 495 in Retail, all four sectors had Searcher 1st and Defender 2nd. Furthermore, in a total sample of 14,537 Females completing the Map, 45 per cent had Searcher 1st, with another 13.2 per cent having Defender in 2nd place.

9 Especially where the range of scores of the nine motivators from top to bottom is large.

10 The I'm NOT OK, You're NOT OK syndrome again, Thomas Harris, ibid.

11 Our preferred methodology for generating a mission statement is included in Chapter 8 of this book.

12 According to Fortune Magazine: http://for.tn/1T3cgwU "Indeed, the Certified Financial Planner Board of Standards says nearly a third of lottery winners declare bankruptcy meaning they were worse off than before they became rich. Other studies show that lottery winners frequently become estranged from family and friends, and incur a greater incidence of depression, drug and alcohol abuse, divorce, and suicide than the average American."

13 *Mapping Motivation for Leadership*, James Sale and Jane Thomas, Routledge (2019).

14 In Chapter 7 we look at the stage-stage process of beliefs to choices, and find here a similar phenomenon, or feedback loop: beliefs affect our choices, but we can also work backwards and consistency of choice can affect beliefs.

15 From the Tao Te Ching. Most religious traditions have something similar. The Bible for example says: "Be still and know that I am God." Psalm 46:10.

16 This comes from Carl Rogers, in *Psychology: A Study of a Science,* volume 3, Formulations of the Persona and the Social Context, edited by S. Koch, McGraw-Hill (1959). More about this is covered in *Mapping Motivation*, James Sale, Routledge (2016).

17 This sounds paradoxical, but we need to see it metaphorically in the same way the acorn is the oak, or the caterpillar is the butterfly; but to get to what they each become they need to go through a process. The acorn, for example, cannot become what it already 'is' (potentially), the oak, without soil, air, water and light. So neither can we without a 'process' of personal development.

18 *The Road to Character*, David Brooks, Random House (2015). This fascinating book explores precisely this theme with a number of outstanding men and women who 'became' astonishing pioneers and leaders despite serious security and success deficiencies in their early life. People such as Frances Perkins, Dwight Eisenhower, Dorothy Day, George Marshall and more, including the great Dr Johnson.

7 Coaching, mapping motivation, and changing values

Everything in life depends upon our beliefs, and the primary reason for this is that they become self-fulfilling prophecies. What we believe – the mental and emotional constructs that the mind forms – becomes either the cage in which we imprison ourselves with our own limitations, real or imagined, or it becomes the clear blue sky in which we can soar, be free – or freer – and realise our full potential. Essentially, beliefs lie at the heart of exceptional performance, but they have to be positive beliefs, aligned with how reality works. Research in Positive Psychology over the last three decades has conclusively shown that the belief, for example, if you work hard then you will be successful, and therefore happy, is entirely erroneous; instead, we learn that if we are happy, then happiness leads to enhanced performance in all fields of our life, including achieving success.[1] Considering how many people operate under the specious 'work hard' belief gives rise to the highly likely suspicion that it is commonplace to operate under false or limiting beliefs.[2]

Before we introduce values, which are an accentuated form of belief, we might like briefly to look at the consequences and sequencing of beliefs themselves, which will help illustrate further why they are so important. Beliefs are the starting point in the chain that leads to our choices; and this chain runs something like this (see Figure 7.1).

We begin with a belief, positive or negative, and this ultimately produces the choices we make in life; these choices develop our character and prove finally to become our destiny (positively) or fate (negatively).[3] To give examples would be the clearest thing here (see Figure 7.2).

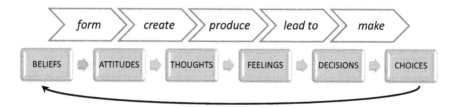

Figure 7.1 Beliefs to choices

	Belief	Attitude	Thought	Feeling	Decision	Choice
+	I am highly able	Optimistic	I can go higher in life	Excitement	To go for promotion	At a larger, more prestigious organisation
-	I'm not good enough	Pessimistic	I mustn't be seen to fail	Boredom	To stay where I am	To carry on as is, not rock the boat

Figure 7.2 Examples of beliefs to choices

With this sequence in mind we can see clearly why beliefs are so important. But notice, too, in Figure 7.1 that choices also feedback into beliefs. This leads onto two observations. First, that if we change our beliefs it will ultimately lead us to make different choices; but equally, if we consistently make certain choices – in other words, form certain habits (which are what consistent choices lead to) – then these will affect our beliefs in a feedback loop. Second, as with memory,[4] the first and last items in a sequence tend to be more important than the items in the middle. So if we want to make the most impact as coaches we are well advised to focus on beliefs, or choices, or both as a matter of priority. Indeed, if we were to be Pareto-about-it, then beliefs and choices are the 30+ per cent that probably lead to the 70 per cent of outcomes, which is why this coaching book has had such a strong focus on beliefs and making the action choices that must follow from them.

But now we come to three special sets of belief. First, what we believe about ourselves; and these beliefs affect our self-concept.[5] This is an overarching term that encompasses our self-esteem, our self-image, and also our ideal self. It's very far reaching in its ramification; we cannot perform beyond how we define our own self-concept. Second, another set of beliefs we call our expectations: these are our beliefs (which may include beliefs about our future self too) that refer to our perspective on how things work and will turn out in the real world. The self-concept and our expectations form the core of what motivates us,[6] and so that is why we place motivation so centrally in personal development work; and it is why low expectations invariably create self-limitations and self-fulfilling prophecies. But, finally, we also have, as a special set of beliefs, those we call our values, and these are critical too.

Our values are beliefs to which we have attached especial importance and significance; and the attachment of this importance and significance to them means that they affect us emotionally. We find it very difficult to be unmoved when one of our core values is challenged or threatened; equally, we rejoice when our values are realised in some way in the real world. Another way of expressing this is to say "a value is a belief in action"[7]; in other words, because the belief is so important to us, it is one we tend to act on or actively seek out. And because there is an especially strong emotional component to values, it should be obvious too that there is a clear link with Motivational Maps. The Maps are not intellectual constructs, but are based on measuring what we want; and in essence are like values, when we realise or fulfil our motivators we become happy and satisfied, and gain even more energy thereby. Indeed, that is what emotion does: e-motion, it moves us, and to be moved and moving requires energy. Values therefore motivate us and you can see this as a coach when you ask someone what is important to them about security, belonging, recognition, control or influence, money, learning and expertise, innovation, autonomy, meaning. You in essence find out the further subconscious values that underpin that motivator for that individual and also the beliefs that cluster around the value. So values and motivators have a synergistic relationship. And these values can be a positive or negative influence in the client's life and they can be creating momentum towards something that they want or away from something which they do not want.

One of the problems with values is that, as with our motivators, we are not always aware of what our values are consciously, and how they can drive our behaviours in ways that are counterproductive to our well-being. Before we go any further, though, it would be good to examine how our motivators may themselves be the foundation stones of some of our values or put another way the values that are underpinning our motivational preferences and how our beliefs underpin our values. In the first instance, let's consider how values and motivators might be aligned (see Figure 7.3).

ACTIVITY 7.1

Consider your top three motivators and review the likely values that we assign to them. Make a list of those you think apply to you. Where in your life are these values being realised? Rank order them now in terms of their importance to you. Draw up a plan in which you propose to work on getting more of the top five 'values' into your life and work.

As we see from Figure 7.2 beliefs can lead to positive or negative 'choices' for us, so it should come as no surprise that our motivators also have a similar potential; context, as we say, is everything. Here are some possible ways in which a given motivator might represent a strong value for an individual, but as a belief could be either positive or negative (see Figure 7.4).

Motivator	Likely Values
Searcher	meaning & purpose in what they do, significant & important work, making a difference, seeing the big picture, being listened to / consulted, change & variety, relevance, learning linked to meaning, avoiding meaninglessness, needing to know why, serving, helping people, vision linked to purpose, avoidance of irrelevance, not doing the mundane, contribution, empowerment, personal fulfilment
Spirit	working autonomously, making own decisions, having a choice, freedom & independence, awareness of the bigger picture, clear & specific objectives, not being micro-managed, not being controlled, control over time, flexibility, not being hemmed in, effectiveness, speed, not being slowed down, avoiding bureaucracy, agility
Creator	environment with change & variety, opportunity to solve problems, being original, creating the new/improved, ability to work alone / small groups, recognition of creativity, innovative, creative, new, challenging, fresh, invigorating, avoidance of the known, ideas, lack of structure, exuberance, energy, colourful, not being stale, not being stuck, not being blocked, not being rigid, not being formal

Motivator	Likely Values
Expert	opportunities to learn, specialisation, sharing expertise, realising own potential, respect for other experts, mastery of own work, professionalism, getting it right, not making mistakes, not being seen to get it wrong, education, development, enhancement, progression
Builder	above average standard of living, material & financial rewards, clear goals & targets, work that is visibly well rewarded, responsibility, competitive/targeted environment, success, winning, providing nice things, specific possessions, not losing, not being shown up, not letting people down
Director	being in control / in charge, being stretched, making critical decisions, clearly-defined career path, having control of resources. responsibility & influence, power, positive impact on others, direction, clarity, impact, career progression, career enhancement, mentoring, not being overruled, not being told what to do, leadership

Figure 7.3a, b and c Values and motivators

Motivator	Likely Values
Star	social & public recognition, being noticed & held in high esteem, awards & certificates, clear hierarchy / pecking order, competitive opportunities, positive feedback, being valued, being recognised, not wanting to be not recognised, praise, adulation, respect, not being ignored, being heard, prestige, titles, standing, reputation, not being tarnished
Friend	feeling of belonging, nourishing & fulfilling relationships, collaborative environment, being liked & supported, being listened to, loyalty & continuity, not being unliked, fitting in, not being seen to be different, fun, friendliness, not being rude, informality, shared experiences, looking after others, not being selfish
Defender	high job security, clear roles & responsibilities, regular & accurate information, continuity & loyalty, order & clarity, time to prepare, stability, the known, not being insecure, not wanting not to know, being sure, planned, reflective, not being uncertain, change for longer term security

Figure 7.3 (Continued)

Motivator	Value	Possible Aligned Belief/Limiting Belief
Defender	Security	It is good to be cautious / Change is threatening
Friend	Belonging	I like contributing / I have to be liked
Star	Recognition	I like to progress / I need to look good
Director	Influence	I like to be decisive / I have to be in control
Builder	Money	It's good to be abundant / I must win at all costs
Expert	Mastery	I like to learn / I don't know enough
Creator	Innovation	I like creating things / Structure is boring
Spirit	Autonomy	I love effectiveness / I am impatient
Searcher	Meaning	I want to make a difference / I won't do meaningless

Figure 7.4 Aligning motivators and potential values

ACTIVITY 7.2

What are your top three motivators? Study Figure 7.4. Examine each possible positive/negative belief/value that may arise from your three motivators. Ask: does the 'positive' belief/value resonate with me? And, if you are being honest, does the 'negative' also reflect something of what you think – what you believe? How are you going to address your potentially negative belief/value? Remember, you are emotionally attached to it.

ACTIVITY 7.3

As a coach, use the table in Figure 7.4 to establish your client's possible belief/values – whilst looking to reinforce positive belief/values and change or reframe negative ones. This can be done by converting all the belief/value statements into questions to see how they respond. Here are some examples (see Figure 7.5).

Of course, so far we have kept the belief/values that derive from the motivators closely aligned with the motivators' central definitions. But we can go beyond these to look at a much wider picture of possible values that we or the client might hold.

Motivator	Positive & Negative Values	Positive, Negative Question
Searcher	can make a difference	How do you know you make a difference?
	good intentions justify means	What do you do when others block your actions?
Spirit	can be effective	How do you respond to challenges?
	don't need anybody else	What do you do when a problem gets too big?
Creator	change is positive	How do you respond to change?
	stability is boring	What happens when there are periods of consolidation?

Figure 7.5a, b and c Positive and negative values and questions

Motivator	Positive & Negative Values	Positive, Negative Question
Expert	education for life	How have you used your training?
	know-it-all already	What learning plans do you have for the year?
Builder	believing in abundance	How do you approach negotiations?
	believing nice 'guys' lose	What's your attitude to less successful colleagues/competitors?
Director	managing for purpose	What are you intending to do and why?
	controlling from ego	What's important to you as a team member?

Motivator	Positive & Negative Values	Positive, Negative Question
Star	achieving status	How important is rank to you?
	assuming superiority	What do you think of people below you?
Friend	wanting to contribute	How important is contributing to you?
	needing to depend	What would you feel if you were disliked at work?
Defender	preferring caution	How cautious do you like to be?
	suspecting innovation	What is your attitude towards innovation?

Figure 7.5 (Continued)

ACTIVITY 7.4

Study the motivators again. What possible, and wider, values might be associated with each one of them. For example, if we think of a wide-ranging value that many people in the West hold as sacred – democracy, for example, or freedom – what motivator might be aligned with them? It would seem obvious to us that the Spirit with its emphasis on autonomy is just such a motivator. What else, perhaps? And go through the other eight motivators exploring where there might be connections to wider values (see Figure 7.6).

No list of values is likely to be complete, but those in Figure 7.6 augment the picture we have drawn of possible motivator values in Figure 7.3. We can say just as we did in Figure 7.5 that there will be relevant coaching questions, as likely values can be probed by the coach: what standards do you apply? How do you manifest consistency? Why is clarity so important to you? And so on.

To elicit your clients' values around their Motivational Preferences we use one question initially and that question is: What is important to you about … see selected word(s) in Figure 7.7 for each motivator.

ACTIVITY 7.5

Ask the client – or yourself – the same question for each of their (or your) top three motivators, or any scoring above 20 points. After each answer ask, what else is important to you about *Security*, until you are sure they have run out of ideas, and make a note of all the words, that is, the values that arise. You may as well wish to consider low motivators scoring below 10 to see whether there are extreme negative values too! Some clients will have negative emotion and limiting beliefs around a value, and others won't. The key is only to change what isn't working for the client. And also, keep in mind, just as skills and motivators may not always be in sync, so the neat compartmentalising of certain values against particular motivators may not always be accurate: for people can always surprise with their own internal contradictions!

Now that you are aware of your client's values around each motivational preference, you may also begin to be aware of which potential values are more likely to cause the client an issue. For example, 'Not Being Slowed Down' or 'Not Being Formal' are what we call away from values[8] where the client subconsciously is focusing on what they do not want, and so are *moving away* from something. This may be a problem, as they may avoid situations where they might otherwise learn something important – but don't learn, for fear of making mistakes. Let's look, then, at the nine motivators and contrast typical *Away from* values with the *Towards* (see Figure 7.8).

So we need to look now at how much the client's motivators involve away from values (which, when we do the value analysis, come out as likely to start with a 'Not …'). We want to know, approximately, and overall, what percentage they are *moving towards* what they want, and what percentage they are *moving away* from what they don't want.

If we take the Expert motivator as an example and ask the question, 'What is important to you about Expertise?', then if they reply 'Learning', the coach will follow on with, 'What is important to you about Learning?' The client may say, 'Self-improvement' (which is a *towards* value), then the coach asks, 'What is important to you about self-improvement?' Suppose the client says, 'not standing still' (which is an *away from* value); so we now have two *towards* and one *away from* values.

So, we ask again, 'What else is important to you about Learning?', and the client might say, 'being a better person'. This sounds like a *towards*, but is actually an *away from* as better implies better than what they don't want. And therefore you ask

Motivator	Possible and Wider Values
SEARCHER	fairness? tolerance? equality? goodness?
SPIRIT	freedom? democracy? directness? autonomy? liberty?
CREATOR	creativity? openness? curiosity? innovation? beauty?
EXPERT	rationality? truth? honesty? knowledge?
BUILDER	competition? challenge? materialism? results?
DIRECTOR	authority? obedience? discipline? power? leadership?
STAR	respect? sociability? hierarchy? fame?
FRIEND	friendship? love? support? consensus? reciprocity? acceptance?
DEFENDER	standards? consistency? clarity? order?

Figure 7.6 Motivators and their possible and wider values

What is Important to you About ...	
Meaning/Purpose	For the Searcher
Autonomy/Freedom	For the Spirit
Innovation	For the Creator
Expertise/Mastery	For the Expert
Money/Competition	For the Builder
Influence/Control	For the Director
Recognition	For the Star
Belonging	For the Friend
Security	For the Defender

Figure 7.7 What is important to you about ...?

again, 'What is important to you about being a better person?' and the client says something like 'not being stuck' (which is an *away from*). You now have two *away from* and two *towards* values, and you keep going until the client runs out or repeats words. The split of *towards* and *away from* answers gives you a sense of whether they are more frequently going for what they want or avoiding what they don't want.

Make a note of all of the *away from* and *towards* answers for each value and share those with the client. Explain the concept of moving either *towards* what you want, or *away from* what you don't want; and then help work out what percentage they are *moving towards* learning and what percentage they are *moving away* from its opposite (that is, not knowing enough). What you will end up with is something like this real case study as shown in Figure 7.9:

Motivational Preference	Towards Values	Away from Values
Searcher	Purpose in life	Avoidance of routines
Spirit	Autonomy	Withdrawing from constraints
Creator	New ideas	Avoiding received ideas
Expert	Learning, development	Not knowing, not being wrong
Builder	Affluence	Avoiding losing what they have
Director	Positive influence	Avoiding others being in control
Star	Legitimate recognition	Not being a nobody
Friend	Good relationships	Not being disliked
Defender	The known, tried and trusted	Away from the uncertain

Figure 7.8 Towards and away from values

Now that we have the client's values and the direction of the energy or motivation for each value, we can begin to unpick what it is that may be underneath the *away from* motivation, and also the potential source of any negative emotion and discomfort for the client (which are any limiting beliefs).

Motivational Preference = EXPERT				
Values	Towards	Away	% towards	% away
Learning	3	2	60%	40%
Professionalism	1	4	20%	80%
Self improvement	4	1	80%	20%
Knowledge	3	2	60%	40%
Not making mistakes	0	5	0%	100%
Overall approximation			45% moving towards what they want 55% moving away from what they do not want	

Figure 7.9 Client Joan: Away/Towards scoring for motivator Expert

ACTIVITY 7.6

Continuing with the thread of the Expert, and the example above, let's now find out how to uncover the limiting beliefs that underpin the issues which may be present. For each value (especially those with *away from* motivation), ask the client:

What do you believe about [each value]?

In Joan's example we would be asking, 'What do you believe about … '

Learning
Professionalism
Self improvement
Knowledge and
Not making mistakes

in turn, and making a note of any beliefs that seem to inhibit our client's success and happiness.

For example, when asking what do you believe about professionalism? You could get the following answers …

It's good to be professional
High standards are important
It's good to get things right
I like getting things right first time
It's important to be seen in a good light by others
It is important to me that I am not seen as unprofessional
It is important that I'm not seen as weak

It is easy here to spot the couple of limiting beliefs, in *italics*; albeit there could be others lurking underneath the seemingly positive statements, and so you have to trust your intuition as a coach. If you suspect that there are limiting beliefs hiding, then, as previously, probe further and ask them, 'What do you believe about the belief it is good to be professional?'

Client: 'It's important for me to get things right first time.'
Coach: 'And what do you believe about that?'
Client: '*People will look down at me if I make mistakes*'

So, from a seemingly positive statement, we find that there is a limiting belief under the surface. Our general advice as coaches is to expect limiting beliefs to be present; that way one is more prepared to be able to significantly help the client.

Where does this lead us? Well, now as a coach we have a lot of very useful information at our fingertips. To summarise:

• Firstly, we have a Motivational Map and a clear indication of which motivational preferences are not being fulfilled currently.

- Secondly, for those preferences at the top of the map not being fulfilled, we have elicited the client's values (what is important to them) about those preferences.
- Thirdly, we know how much the client is *moving towards* what they want and *away from* what they do not want for each value, and the motivational preference as a whole.
- Finally, we have the client's limiting beliefs that underpin the value and the direction of the energy/motivation of that value.

ACTIVITY 7.7

How are we going to address a belief that isn't working for us? Remember, we are emotionally attached to it, and the likelihood is that when we think about the negative aspect there will be subtle or not so subtle negative emotion which goes with it. The question we have to ask is: 'What is a better feeling-thought than the one we have?' A 'feeling-thought' being a thought that generates feelings in us – which is what strong beliefs and values do.

We believe, say:

Nice guys lose	(so improve this feeling-thought)
Nice guys feel good when they do what is right	
	(so improve this feeling-thought)
When they do what is right, they win because they feel good	
	(keep going)
Feeling good ultimately is successful in its own right	(keep going)
I sell more effectively when I feel good	(keep going)
To be effective I need to feel good, and if being nice	
helps me achieve that, then being nice is winning!	(an enabling belief)

Or another example:

Menial tasks are beneath me	(so improve this feeling-thought)
I need to get certain things done that I might not like doing	
	(keep going)
It's only me who decides whether I enjoy something or not	
	(keep going)
All activities in life are neutral; it is me who puts the energy into it	
	(keep going)
I can practise being mindful in doing tasks I have previously resisted	
	(keep going)
It will be good for people around me to see me getting stuck in	
	(keep going)
I am going to commit to doing what needs to be done and enjoy it as it	
will lead to greater meaning in the longer term!	(an enabling belief)

Take a belief or value that isn't working for you (or do it with your client) and ask: 'What is a better feeling-thought than the one I have?' Improve it in the way we have indicated.

To build further on this, it is possible using NLP techniques to make one value more important and another less important. This can be extremely useful for a client if that value isn't serving the client. In Joan's example, letting go of 'not making mistakes' and making that whole value less important will have two impacts: one, it will make her move more *towards* what she wants rather than *away from* what she doesn't want. To do this one might give her a task that links to that desired change: like creating something in draft form, which she knows isn't perfect, and asking for feedback on that experience.

How does this work? Well, in NLP we understand that each experience, value and belief is coded subconsciously in a symbolic way. Everything in our subconscious has a specific code of modalities: visual, auditory (sounds or no sound) and kinaesthetic (feelings), or VAK for short. The combinations of ways we can store things via our sub-modalities are potentially limitless. Whenever we re-experience a memory, we do so in our mind's eye with a combination of specific VAK sub-modalities (see Figure 7.10).

Our unique subconscious coding of our experience occurs through our modalities (visual/auditory/kinaesthetic), and a good way of thinking about this is as if it were a subconscious bar code. If we change the bar code, we change the meaning for the client.

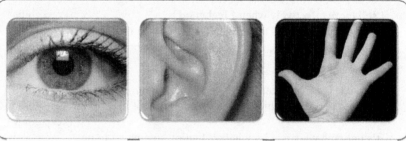

Visual	Auditory	Kinaesthetic
• Black and white or colour	• Loud or soft	• Internal or external
• Near or far/specific location	• Inside or external	• Location in the body
• Bright or dim	• Uniqueness of sound	• Size
• Movie or a still		• Shape
• Framed or panoramic		• Pressure
• Looking through your own eyes or seeing yourself in a picture		• Weight
• Big or small		• Temperature
		• Vibration

Figure 7.10 VAK sub-modalities[9]

ACTIVITY 7.8

Revisit that limiting belief/value again. What is it? Make sure you are nice and relaxed.

Close your eyes and consider, when you think about that belief: do you have a picture? Notice what you see, hear and feel. Once you have an image, however clear or otherwise, change it to be small, dark and in the distance. Ask yourself: is this more or less compelling here? If it is less compelling, make it even further way, so that it becomes even less so, till eventually irrelevant; then bring yourself back to now and open your eyes.

If the image becomes more compelling in the distance, bring it back to where it was previously, and move it behind you or in some position in relation to your body that makes it feel less compelling to you, and which feels more comfortable. Aim to find the location on the screen of your mind's eye that makes it feel the most comfortable and the least compelling for you, and then bring yourself back to now and open your eyes.

Figure 7.11 The mind's eye and near and far images

ACTIVITY 7.9

Go through exactly the same process as before, except this time notice if you are looking through your own eyes or seeing yourself in the picture? If you are looking through your own eyes, change it so that you are seeing yourself in the picture, and notice if that is less compelling and feels more comfortable. If it does, then leave the image as it is, and bring yourself quickly back to the present moment.

The purpose of these exercises is not so much to make a huge difference to your quality of life immediately, as changing beliefs and values fully requires either intense and prolonged practice or expert assistance from a coach. But, instead, this is more about providing a taster for you to understand that you can change limiting beliefs and values; and doing so, in turn, will affect our motivators as well. We will spot the shift next time we do our Motivational Map. It may be the order of the motivators has changed, or the intensity (reflected in the scoring) has altered.

Before we go any further we might want to ask ourselves where our values and beliefs come from anyway? In a sense this should be obvious from some of the Case Study examples we have used throughout the book. But in essence our beliefs about our self – our self-concept – develop throughout our life, though it is in childhood that its foundations are laid. We form our identity in response to the environment in which we find ourselves, and in particular in response to the 'hypnosis'[10] or conditioning that occurs through the primary medium of parental (or carer) messaging – what we are told over and over again by our parents at a young age tends to stick in our minds, for good or ill, and become habituated as a core belief which we perceive as the 'truth'[11] – about ourselves and about reality.

We say 'hypnosis' because in a strange way that is exactly what it is[12]. The reason for this is to do with brain wave patterns that develop as we grow up. Adults, typically in their waking hours, experience what is called beta brain wave patterns (vibrating at a frequency of c. 13–35 Hz); this reflects ordinary, everyday, busy thinking. But when we become relaxed, or meditate, we sink into alpha (c.8–12 Hz); this is a state in which learning, memory and healing is enhanced. If we go into an even deeper state of trance, theta, (c.4–8 Hz), then we cross over into that hypnotic area where creativity, insight and dreams occur. Finally, when we go below this to delta brain wave patterns (0.5–4 Hz) we are in deep sleep. So every adult goes through all four stages/frequencies every day as they go into and come out of sleep; and they can also access these alternative frequencies by practices such as meditation and hypnosis. But, the key thing is, beta is the adult dominant state. However, this is not true for children: children, aged up to 2 years old are dominantly in delta, which is why they sleep so much. Children aged from 2 up to 6 are predominantly in theta, which is why they are so playful, curious and creative. And children between 6–12 years (or puberty) are dominantly in alpha, which is why we all remember so vividly what happened to us at that period of our life. But certainly up to the age of 6, since we are not dominantly in either beta (thinking/judging) or alpha (learning) mode, but actually in the most potentially hypnotic state of all – theta – we are all prime candidates to absorb the messages that parents and others give us. Therefore, it's not like being an adult, where we can possibly resist messages through the critical thinking that is represented in beta; no, the child is hypnotised into believing what its parents communicate to him or her, and there is little they can do to resist these powerful influences.

If we absorb these messages – beliefs – and they are limiting, not in our best interests, and not truly representative of who we are, then clearly we stop being 'whole'. We stop being entirely authentic; instead, we develop inner conflicts. Children start off worry-free and novelty-friendly, but as they grow (most) increasingly worry more, conform more and lose their spontaneity.

And the Pareto Principle[13], or 80/20 Rule, applies here as in every other area of our life. Many events happen to us and their long-term significance is small; but a few incidents have an impact out of all significance to their apparent importance or even duration. Being reprimanded, mocked, ridiculed just once can have an inordinate long-term impact on the young and impressionable mind; equally, repeated castigations, tellings-off, reminders that one is wrong, or not as good as, or imperfect in some way can have seriously deleterious effects both in the immediate present and the longer term future.[14] These 'Significant Emotional Events' play a key part in our life, and as we grow up the subconscious mind tries to protect us from their emotional pain.

One important consequence of this process is that the protection that the subconscious mind affords can take the form of self-sabotage. This means that we have visions, missions, goals and we even state them, write them down, and claim we want them; but at some deeper level within us, we fear success, we do not believe we are worth or worthy of great achievement, so that at some point along the road to what we want our self-sabotage kicks in, we do something completely at variance with what we purport to want or to believe, and we destroy the very possibility of gaining what we think to have. This is particularly evident and relevant in personal relationships. People say they want somebody to love and be loved by, or they claim to love somebody, but then, just as the relationship is going well, they do something – like jarringly criticising the 'beloved' – which scuppers it.

But where in your professional career, job or role is self-sabotage occurring?

ACTIVITY 7.10

Make a list of all the areas where in work or business or your role, you can see that you, or others around you, self-sabotage.

Identify the top three areas – by which we mean the top three most problematic areas where if one self-sabotages it causes maximum distress and problems for you or others.

Key areas that we identify and have seen in our professional work include:

Public speaking
Venturing an opinion
Contradicting or expressing disagreement
Taking a risk
Showing emotion
Offending someone else or not being liked
Non-conformity
Trusting others
Leaving one's comfort zone
Fear of flying

To counter these patterns there are three processes we recommend. The first is self-awareness and its cultivation in oneself. This chapter alone has many ways to explore your values and beliefs that are highly specific. It takes time but it is definitely worth doing. Of course, using a coach to help you can massively accelerate that process and our Resources section gives details of leading Mapping Motivation coaches throughout the world. The Motivational Maps themselves, of course, we see as a core resource in raising self-awareness.

Second, is to develop the ability to live in the present moment. This is an ancient Buddhist and Christian principle, and in the West has been popularised by Eckhart Tolle[15] and John Main.[16] We looked at ways of stilling the mind in Chapter 4 when we considered Activity 4.1 and Activity 4.2, the Breathing and the Hakalua Stillness Exercises. These – or alternatives[17] – need to be done regularly, and keep in mind that in doing them we also help slow our brain wave patterns from beta to alpha, and this has many benefits, including health, learning and insight.

Finally, we need to understand that the three great change tools in the human psyche are:

a   Our desires
b   Our expectations
c   Our imagination[18]

These three tools drive us to make changes in our life. If we consider them, we see how much we already have covered. First, our desires are what we want. If we want something enough we become focused on achieving it; but we have to want *enough*. And this is why throughout we have advocated feeding our motivators, for these too are what we want. So, the first step is to need to want to change! And we want to change because we want to improve, to progress, to self-actualise and become all we could be. As David Brook expresses it: "Character is built in the course of your inner confrontation".[19]

Expectations, of course, as we've said, are our beliefs about future outcomes, and throughout we have stressed the importance of positive expectations because these definitely affect results.[20] We have also looked extensively at how we might go about changing our beliefs and values, and hence expectations, in order to create a more positive, optimistic and successful re-orientation.

Finally, what of imagination, perhaps the defining characteristic of being human. How can this help us change for the better?

ACTIVITY 7.11

One application is daydreaming and asking 'what if?'. Visualise yourself with knowledge, skills, talents that appeal to you. By focusing your mind on what you want or even on finding what you want, a powerful force is unleashed. When will you visualise your possibilities? How? Under what conditions?

The power of the imagination is virtually unlimited. Everything that *is* came into existence via the imagination; it was seen in the mind's eye before it was 'created', literally or physically. Thus, the more time is spent imagining ideal realities, the more likely it is that that reality will come to pass.[21] Naturally, it is important that when using visualisation and imaging techniques that we stay in a relaxed state of mind; and note that by doing so we are helping to counter the childhood 'hypnosis' (and its brain wave frequencies) with its own antidote in later life, which are those same lower frequencies.

Finally, in this chapter, where do these three tools themselves derive from? And the strange answer is from our dreams. Our dreams, as we have already noted, occur in sleep when we are in the theta brain wave pattern,[22] which is also responsible for the playful, creative, and curious attitude that we find in children aged 2–6. Other missing words here might include 'intuition' and 'insight'; a deeper level of mind. What is strange is that from such unprepossessing, insubstantial, evanescent materials the reality of our lives is built. Therefore, we need to pay attention to our dreams and what they are trying to tell us. Writing about dreams would be a book in itself, but the simple idea of keeping a log by one's bedside and jotting down any dreams that one recalls on awakening can lead to profound insights. Many people say that they cannot remember any dreams or that they never have any. But research indicates the opposite: we all dream, and if we ask our subconscious mind to remember them as we awake, we find it starts to comply with that habit!

Summary

1 Beliefs become self-fulfilling prophecies.
2 Beliefs ultimately determine our choices in life, though choices can affect our beliefs.
3 Values are beliefs which are both important to us and which emotionally resonate with us.
4 Values are often subconscious, like our motivators, to which they are also connected.

5   Our values tend to have a direction either towards what we want or moving away from what we do not want.
6   The beliefs we have around each value can be either empowering or disabling.
7   Changing limiting beliefs changes our perception and our choices.
8   Changing our values changes what is important to us and what motivates us.
9   We can counter negative values and beliefs engrained in early childhood by accessing, through visualisation and imagination, deeper levels of mind.

Notes

1   *The Happiness Advantage*, Shawn Achor, Crown Business (2010), gives a comprehensive account of some of the research in this area.
2   Another classic error we have already covered in Chapter 3: Pareto - that people believe that inputs to outputs are 50/50, when they are more likely to be 80/20.
3   This six-stage progression of beliefs to choices is found in a wide range of literature on the topic, including: *An Awakening: Mapping Your Dream* Volume 1, Suzanne Hosang, Dog Ear Publishing (2011) and *5 Steps to a Quantum Life: How to Use the Astounding Secrets of Quantum Physics to Create the Life You Want*, Natalie Reid, Winged Horse Publishing (2007).
4   As Tony Buzan put it, summarising the research, "the human brain primarily remembers the following: items from the beginning of the learning period ('the primacy effect') ... items from the end of the learning period ('the recency effect') ...", *The Mind Map Book*, Tony Buzan, BBC Books (1993/5).
5   For more on the self-concept and Carl Rogers' view of it see Chapter 2, The Roots of Motivation, *Mapping Motivation*, James Sale, Gower (2016).
6   A detailed account of this occurs in *Mapping Motivation*, James Sale, Gower (2016), Chapter 2.
7   *The Fish Rots from the Head*, Bob Garratt, HarperCollins (1997).
8   This concept is commonly referred to in NLP literature, for example, *NLP: The New Technology of Achievement*, Steve Andreas and Charles Faulkner, Nicholas Brealey (1998), but ultimately derives from Freud (Project for a Scientific Psychology, 1895) and his ideas of moving away from pain and towards pleasure.
9   Note that these are just a selection and not a comprehensive list. Also note, there is a fourth modality in NLP called Auditory Digital (or Ad) that relates to our inner dialogue or self-talk, but in order to keep things simple and manageable we have not explored it further in this book.
10   "The most influential perceptual programming of the subconscious mind occurs from birth through age six." - Dr Bruce Lipton, *Are You Programmed at Birth? How to Transform the Subconscious Trance* (2010), http://bit.ly/2tINYih.
11   As Martin Seligman put it, "It is essential to realise that your beliefs are just that - beliefs. They may or may not be facts", *Authentic Happiness*, Random House, Australia (2002).
12   "Delta and theta brain frequencies define a brain state known as a hypnagogic trance- the same neural state that hypnotherapists use to directly download new behaviors into the subconscious minds of their clients. In other words, the first six years of a child's life are spent in a hypnotic trance!" Bruce Lipton, ibid.
13   The Pareto Principle: one of the best books on the Pareto Principle and its applications for organisations and business is Richard Koch: *The 80/20 Principle and the Secret of Achieving More with Less* (2007).
14   Though one should not lose sight of the fact that negative experiences can also galvanise one to outstanding performances subsequently. A good example is that of George Catlett Marshall (of The Marshall Plan fame) who, after overhearing his brother tell

their mother that George would 'disgrace the family name' was so affected that he developed an 'urgency to succeed' that never left him. Cited by David Brooks, *The Road to Character*, Random House (2015).

15 Eckhart Tolle, *The Power of Now*, Yellow Kite (2001).

16 John Main, *The Inner Christ*, Darton Longman Todd (1987).

17 Stilling the mind does not just mean 'sitting' down! Yoga is a practical discipline that has these benefits, as does Chi Gung and Tai Chi. Indeed, Tai Chi is often called a 'moving meditation'.

18 Lee Pulos, *The Biology of Empowerment*, Nightingale Conant (2005).

19 David Brooks, *The Road to Character*, ibid.

20 "Expecting positive outcomes actually makes them more likely to arise" - Shawn Achor, *The Happiness Advantage*, Crown Business (2010).

21 GK Chesterton noted, "At least in the mind of man, if not in the nature of things, there seems to be some connection between concentration and reality".

22 "Theta brain waves are present during deep meditation and light sleep, including the all-important REM dream state." *This Is How Brain Waves Contribute to the State of Mind*, Mind Valley Academy Blog (2017), http://bit.ly/2pBaatc.

8   Career coaching

One of the most obvious applications of the Motivational Map is with career coaching. With so many people considering career moves and life changes often decisions can be made on a whole variety of factors including, financial, geographic, familial and of course emotional. Very few people considering a change in their career review their subconscious values and seek a decision that is 100 per cent aligned; keeping in mind, of course, that values and, even more so, beliefs can change over time!

Here is where the Motivational Map helps us – to find what precisely is motivating us in our career right now, how we feel our work is meeting our needs right now, and how our values are likely to change over time.

This point about 'changing' over time is significant because it means that Maps resist stereotyping people in the way a psychometric tool will often do. That said, however, it should come as no surprise to learn that certain professions tend to have certain Map profiles, and when we consider our career choices it's as well to keep that point in mind. Research done by us on more than 28,000 people across 144 sectors clearly shows a number of things.

Here is, in Figure 8.1, a cross-section of 10 sectors[1] with their top three motivators, and the sample size on which the rank ordering is based. Clearly, the numbers can be finessed further to take account of nationality, age, role and gender,[2] but even as they stand they are striking. Most striking of all being the fact that all 10 sectors have Searcher[3] – the need to make a difference – as their number one motivator. In a way this entirely validates two other pieces of information: first, the view that people do not simply want to work for money. True, in Banking it (the Builder) appears as the third most important, but that's all. Second, Simon Sinek wrote a book called *Start with Why*.[4] He argued that organisations had become too preoccupied with *What* they do and *How* they do it; this was largely de-motivating for staff because what employees wanted was a big WHY – why are we doing this to get them out of bed in the morning. Our research[5] shows that Sinek's point is true: making a difference is the outcome of mission or purpose, the central concern of the Searcher motivator.

The other noticeable thing about Figure 8.1 is that four whole motivators are not mentioned at all in these statistics; they are mentioned in some of the other 134 sectors we have covered, but much less so. They are, for want of a better word, rarer! What are these motivators? They are the Friend,[6] the Director, the Creator, and, in fact the least frequent of all, the Star.[7] Some fascinating, if not worrying, ideas emerge from this: first, the fact that people generally are not inclined to want

Sector	Motivator			
	1	2	3	Sample Size
Accounting	Searcher	Defender	Spirit	432
Banking	Searcher	Defender	Builder	204
Computer Software	Searcher	Expert	Spirit	232
Construction	Searcher	Expert	Defender	634
Education Management	Searcher	Expert	Defender	1673
Government Admin	Searcher	Expert	Defender	592
Hospital & Health Care	Searcher	Defender	Expert	675
Human Resources	Searcher	Spirit	Expert	606
Pharmaceuticals	Searcher	Expert	Defender	437
Retail	Searcher	Defender	Expert/Spirit=	495
Telecommunications	Searcher	Expert	Spirit	188

Figure 8.1 Map data for a cross-section of employment sectors

to belong to an organisation, or indeed do not desire to manage it.[8] But secondly, if your Map profile is high in these four lesser desired motivators, how can you be sure you will thrive in a sector environment that maybe does not operate or respect their particular energies? This, again, is why knowing your Motivational Map is key to your career development, and key for coaches seeking to help their clients.

Of special note is the absence of the Creator motivator in the light of the fact that business turns on the reality of innovation: people may have innovative skills and knowledge but if they don't actually desire innovation, then they will always default to some other activity that pleases them more – and satisfies a motivator they do want. The implications of this, especially in recruitment, really need addressing.

One final point is that three of the four 'rarer' motivators – Friend, Star, and Director – actually are sequential on the Map hierarchy, and they share some common properties. Of significance here is that Friend and Star are Relationship motivators, and although Director is an Achievement motivator, yet being on the border of Relationship, it often requires relationships to function. In other words, to want to manage people does itself require we develop relationships too. Thus, taking all three together, we would appear to have in a way a chronic absence of effective relationship-building motivators. The net effect of this would be, if a larger data-set substantiated this finding, an overemphasis, perhaps, on transactional relationships at the expense of transformational ones. Again, as with the Creator motivator, the potential implications for business are wide-ranging.

Before we get onto a case study this all leads to another career issue, especially given the prevalence in our culture today of the Searcher motivator. Earlier we referred to knowing what one's mission – your mission – is in life; but how do we know what it is or ascertain it? This is not the same as vision, that ideal state we aspire to in the future, or values, which are our most deeply held beliefs. It is more about what were you – we – born to do?

This is not an easy question, and it may take some considerable teasing out. Coaching is an ideal methodology for helping anybody get greater clarity on this issue; that much should be obvious if only because of the profound questions coaching asks, and which we looked at in Chapter 1. But the Motivational Map has its own techniques to help address this issue.

The key thing to understand about Mission[9] is that it is about finding out what we 'do'; we go on at length in our culture about each individual being unique, but then we seek to package them just like everybody else in a standard job. This, perhaps, more than anything else is why most surveys estimate that approximately two-thirds of the work force in the USA and the UK, and other countries too, are disengaged. Employees are *doing* things that do not bring out their unique gifts and talents – or draw on what they were born to do.

When we say 'do', then, it may remind us that in every full sentence in the English language there is what is sometimes familiarly called a 'doing' word; it is the verb, in fact. And here is our first clue. If we truly want to know what defines us, what is the verb that I associate more than any other with myself, that best describes me?

Verbs are the strong words; but you need to be aware that there are thousands of them, and that they include such 'fuzzy' ideas as 'dreaming' – to dream is a verb. So in doing this exercise we don't have to, at this stage, choose words that are hard-edged. No, at this stage we are investigating where our own true interests lie.

Here are some examples of words/verbs[10] to give a range of ideas:

> *help build organise lead sing teach nurse create administer manage write inspire design encourage solve detect construct paint think imagine repair play run negotiate direct run jump compete collaborate …*

and whatever else comes to mind.

ACTIVITY 8.1

Write down the three most likely verbs that you think apply to you. To establish what they are, you may wish to reflect on your earlier years, especially when people commented on how well you did something that you thought easy and natural – 'can't everyone do this?' The other quality of this thing you did was you found it relatively easy. When you have established three verbs, then brood on them for a while before deciding which one is *your* verb. You may ask two or three people who are close to you for feedback to ensure you have chosen correctly.

Given the relevance of this verb to your life and well-being, the question now is: how much of this verb do you do? How can you do more?

Having established what your verb is, we can go on to create our mission statement. A mission statement is a short paragraph at most that sets out what you do, and we like it when it covers the three bases of our Relationships, our Achievements and our Growth. In this way we align our life, not just even our work, with our mission.

ACTIVITY 8.2

To help us do that, here are four good questions to consider before writing a statement:

i   What do you want to do before you die?
ii   What do you never want to do again?
iii What do you want to offer and contribute?
iv   How do you want to change, develop and grow?

Take some time to complete and jot down your answers to these questions.

You are now in a position to create your own mission statement. This self-same exercise was done by co-author James some years ago. He discovered – to his surprise – that 'to motivate' was indeed his verb. Surprise because, yes, even as a teenager he had had the ability to motivate and energise others around him, though at the time had not considered this significant or important in any way.

James' Mission Statement based on his verb, 'motivate', is:

The focus of my life is to motivate others; it starts with ensuring that I am motivated myself at all times. It extends to my family, friends and the groups I come into contact with. And my work is to increase people's motivation throughout the world by creating processes, systems, ideas that others can use, enjoy, and develop to their own great advantage. To become so motivated I am enthused in its original meaning: 'god-breathed'.

Notice how this mission statement covers his own development, as well as family and work. Notice, too, how once it has been formulated it can be the bench mark for all James' activities: is he motivating in the way he suggests he has been called to do? And notice how the mission statement has an element of "being" in it: that James himself has to be motivated to live his mission, and that this therefore is a crucial element of a mission. A goal or vision is usually an end outcome, as opposed to a statement about how you will be each and every day; so you can hold yourself accountable to your own mission, and have others do that for you!

ACTIVITY 8.3

Write a short statement of what you understand your mission to be. Use the verb that you have identified as yours. Make it simple, sincere and insist it is... YOU[11]! Post it somewhere where it is always highly visible to you. Check how your life currently covers – or not – the doing of 'it'. Write some mini-missions or short-term plans to help you get more balance in your life and work.

Finally, before looking at case studies it would be good to consider, since we are thinking about your career development, what are employers actually looking for? Different organisations will have different emphases and priorities, but we think that there are about 10 key aspects, and they are almost certainly – Pareto again (so 2 or 3 out of these 10 points will be crucial) – hierarchical. These factors are in possible rank order:

1. Energy[12] and initiative – and here we know motivation is energy
2. Consistent upward trend – or, promotion – are you progressing in your career?
3. Comparable accomplishments to date – or groundwork pointing in that direction
4. Experience, education, background, cultural fit – are you suitable?
5. Problem solving and thinking skills – suggesting agility and strategic nous
6. Talent, competency, knowledge, skills, potential
7. Managerial and organisational competence
8. Team qualities – including motivating others
9. Character[13] – integrity, honesty, resilience, commitment, values
10. Personality – will yours comply with or complement theirs?

In all these 10 factors of employment, the employer is always looking for 'more' of them! So, they want to know that the candidate has more energy (or initiative or motivation) than the other competitors; that the upward trend of their career is superior to another's trajectory; that – to go lower in the list – some aspect of their character or personality, other things (e.g. honesty) being equal, is better than your rivals also applying for the post. But of course, in making a decision, employers usually consider a balance of factors, so whereas you may be manifestly weaker in a certain area, say, your experience or education, this may well be offset by your superior energy, or talent, and this may count for more with the potential employer. Whether they are explicitly aware of it or not, they too will be operating under Pareto Principles – two or three factors will be critical for them. Your job in advance is to know which ones, and ensure you can score strongly in those factors.

ACTIVITY 8.4

Take a look at Figure 8.2[14]. Give yourself a score for each category, 5 being high and 1 being low. If you have done a Motivational Map, then you can certainly use it to ascertain whether you are a 5 or not: 5 would be > 80 per cent and 1 would be < 20 per cent. You should from this analysis get a strong idea of where you are strong and where not. Make a plan to see what Factors you can strengthen, or work round – how can you show yourself in the best possible light?

With these ideas and tools now firmly in the forefront of our thinking about career development, we return to the use of the Motivational Map and its applications. On completing a Map, clients receive a 15-page report, which is detailed, useful and interesting for them; but coaches receive also a 1-page report with what we call the '22 numbers'. No text, just the numbers; and these are so revealing.

FACTORS		1	2	3	4	5	SCORE
1	Energy and initiative						
2	Consistent upward trend						
3	Comparable accomplishments to date						
4	Experience, education, background, cultural fit						
5	Problem solving and thinking skills						
6	Talent, competency, knowledge, skills, potential						
7	Managerial and organisational competence						
8	Team qualities						
9	Character						
10	Personality						

Figure 8.2 Employment factors

Case Study 1

Jake

In 2012 Jake dissatisfied with his then current career asked Bevis to coach him. The 22 numbers of the report look like this (see Figure 8.3):

Analysis for Jake: Raw Results

Motivator	Score	PMA Score / 10
Creator	27	1
Defender	25	1
Friend	22	2
Spirit	22	2
Searcher	21	2
Expert	20	4
Director	16	3
Builder	15	1
Star	12	3
PMA Score	11%	
Cluster Importance		
Relationship (R)	33%	
Achievement (A)	28%	
Growth (G)	39%	

Figure 8.3 Jake's 22 numbers

ACTIVITY 8.5

Understanding the Coach Report

Take a look at the 22 numbers in Figure 8.3. Can you see how the 22 numbers are made up? 9 Score numbers + 9 PMA score numbers + 1 PMA % score + 3 cluster importance numbers = 22 numbers in total. Before we unpack some of the meaning of these numbers, try and work on them yourself.[15]

What do you think, then, are some important points from this that Bevis might want to feedback to Jake?

Some key points to pick out and use in a coaching session:

1 Client is 11 per cent motivated – astonishingly low and worrying for long-term well being
2 Client's top motivator, the Creator, currently only 1/10 satisfied, the lowest possible score
3 Not one motivator, whether significant (> 20) or not to Jake, scores 6/10, the average – so Jake is in a very bad place motivationally and emotionally regarding his work

This extreme result actually made preparation for the coaching session quite straight forward. Following his plan to build rapport, ask open questions about specific motivators (note: The Builder motivator is not important, but a satisfaction score of 1/10 indicates that Jake is dissatisfied with the money he earns), and focus on the main thing: namely, his client's dissatisfaction with his top motivator, The Creator.

In essence one question was incredibly useful during the session and that was: "In the context of your career how is your ability to *work creatively, to be able to innovate and make changes* going for you right now?"

Bevis was able to weave that question in numerous times, coming back to it even when seemingly dealing with other motivators.

ACTIVITY 8.6

Reviewing your Motivational Map

Look at your own unique 15-page Motivational Map. On page 6 take note of the motivational preferences that scored 20+ (your strong motivational preferences) and ask yourself the following questions:

> *How is that going for me right now?*

For example, if Defender were scored 20+ then, "How are you feeling in terms of your levels of security and stability in your work right now?" This question probes the possible fulfilment of this Defender motivational preference. Follow-up questions might be:

> *What could change or improve for me right now to improve motivation in that area?*

> *What needs to stay the same for me to maintain a good level of motivation?*

> *Is there anything you need to communicate openly to improve your own levels of fulfilment?*

Make a note of your answers in Figure 8.4.

Motivational Preferences > 20	Pointers to improve personal motivation
e.g. Defender – want more security	

Figure 8.4 Improving personal motivation

These questions elicited the fact that Jake had left a job 8 years previously after being overlooked for promotion; he'd left, in his own words, in a fit of pique, a job that he truly loved. Yes, he'd gone on to make more money but had become increasingly disenchanted by it. This is a classic case: the whole Builder motivator – being commercial, competitive and materialistic – wasn't really a driver for him, but he had fallen into the trap of chasing something that he imagined, falsely, was.

Inner career conflicts

The session and the Map also flagged up an internal career conflict. We have seen this before in Chapter 6 when we considered 'people' as our block and how we may perceive others as a result. But, whilst a conflict may lead to procrastination and indecision, if we look at Figure 8.1 again we see internal conflicts are typical; So note, for example, how frequently the pairing of Defender and Searcher occurs. Before returning to the specifics of Jake's case study, we might ask, why is this? And the answer is not hard to find: it is the fact that we as humans are often on a paradoxical knife-edge whereby the tension drawing us in two different directions can sometimes be the very 'stretch' we need to have high performance in a given field or sector. Hence, if we take the first sector listed in Figure 8.1, Accounting, and consider what might make a good accountant, then it is not hard to see that Searcher, with its strong customer-focus, is necessary in a service-based type of sector; but then so is Defender with its need to be safe and secure, to get the figures right. They are definitely opposite types of motivator, but in the real world of accounting, they both can be powerful drivers. The consequence of saying this, of course, is that we, as coaches, are not simplistically trying to sort out client's internal 'conflicts' – or at least not where the conflict may work for them or be advantageous in a given role. The conflict may be a good or a bad thing. Again, context is everything.

So, with that in mind, how would or did Jake reconcile the fact that he wanted innovation and change (the Creator motivator) and yet was closely scored with the desire to be stable and secure – to avoid change in other words (the Defender)!

Jake admitted part of him wanted to relax and have a steady job with a good work–life balance; and part of him wanted to strive to be innovative and creative and to be constantly doing new things in new ways. Following the principles and questioning techniques outlined in Chapters 1, 4 and 5 especially, Bevis discovered that Jake's dilemma was deep rooted: his mother and father had split up when he was a teenager. His dad was a tradesman who enjoyed a good work–life balance; but his Mum was much more driven and wanted to achieve. This conflict in the home Jake had taken on subconsciously.

Naturally, seeing this clearly for the first time was a revelation to Jake, as was the fact that further questioning revealed that his whole life to date had seen him stuck between a stable lifestyle and a high-flying job, never fully committing to either, and therefore constantly feeling torn. No wonder his performance at work had suffered alongside his work–life balance.

The task, then – the action that Bevis coaxed him towards – would now be linked directly to his motivational preferences: where could he find work which would both allow him opportunity for innovation and creativity yet at the same time provide security and good relationships?

Jake spoke to his former boss at Headline Radio in Ambershire and accepted his old job back! Less than a year later Jake's boss moved onto bigger and better things, and Jake was promoted to head Headline Radio – both enjoying his role, and having his core motivators met. A great outcome from a coaching intervention.

The most common internal motivational conflicts are outlined in Figures 6.4 and 6.5 in Chapter 6. Let's consider them now in terms of career development.

ACTIVITY 8.7

Take a look at your own Motivational Map and note whether you have any of the opposing motivators together at the top of your map (any motivators scored 20+). If you have, can you see how this might at times make you feel? Or, has this affected your actions at work in any way? Or, specifically do you sense that you procrastinate about certain issues? Again, if the answer is yes to this last question, check what the difference in score is between the two motivators where the tension exists. If the scores are very close it is likely (but not certain) that the feeling, or action, or procrastination might be the more intense. Indeed, the closer together the motivators are in terms of score the greater the chance of internal conflict there will be.

For example, someone with a Defender score of 35 and a Spirit score of 20 is going to experience scarcely any conflict in that area, as clearly security is *much more* important to them. However, someone who has a Defender Score of 26 and a Spirit score of 25 may be much more likely to be experiencing conflict internally. That is, part of me wants security and part of me wants freedom – which is as much as to say, part of me wants no risk (security) and part of me of loves risk (which freedom always entails).

But as we have said, there is a caveat to all this, in that it is entirely possible that there is internal conflict that may be met by the job or role. For example, using the Defender/Spirit tension, the client says: "Well I work for a secure organisation and my manager gives me plenty of autonomy within my role". Voila! Perfect – we don't want to change that then. And this reminds us that there is no 'wrong' Map; only context determines what is suitable.

Guidance, therefore, for both map coaches and individuals means we must check out the possibility of internal conflict rather than presume its presence, even when conflicting motivators appear together in a map. But note as well there is a further clue in the PMA score: for, if there is internal conflict going on with the client, the PMA is likely to be negatively affected, which is to say, low. Conversely if the PMA scores are high, even if the conflicting motivators are present and close together, it suggests that the individual is fulfilling both motivators and that conflict is being resolved in some way.[16]

What if there is internal conflict within my map?

Well, the first thing is not to panic; this is quite natural as we change and our values evolve around work and life changes. And as we have seen, it is entirely possible to find jobs and roles that thrive on these tensions. The key thing is to develop the necessary self-awareness about them, so that we don't get wrong-sided by them. Let's take another real example, then, to work through.

Case Study 2

Leon

Leon came for assistance with his career, whilst he co-owned a highly successful business in London. A relatively recent dad with a young family and a wife who didn't hail from England, he had become conflicted with what he had built and with what he now wanted. His business partner, a good friend, was struggling to understand Leon's desire for change.

ACTIVITY 8.8

Reviewing Leon's 22 numbers

Before we begin our analysis of these numbers, take a look (see Figure 8.5): What do you make of them? What three things are most striking about them? How would you frame feedback or questioning as a result? Also, see if you can identify potentially opposing motivators that are scored 20+.

Analysis for Leon: Raw Results

Motivator	Score	PMA Score / 10
Spirit	28	5
Searcher	24	9
Builder	23	9
Director	22	7
Star	20	6
Friend	18	9
Defender	18	10
Expert	17	9
Creator	10	4

PMA Score	66%	

Cluster Importance		
Relationship (R)	31%	
Achievement (A)	34%	
Growth (G)	35%	

Figure 8.5 Leon's 22 numbers

One of the secrets of Motivational Mapping is to realise that *things change* over time. More specifically, given that the Maps' hierarchy is correlated with the Maslow Hierarchy of Needs,[17] then over time there is a normal or usual propensity for people to ascend the hierarchy. The same is true for Maps. A typical example would be multi-millionaires who clearly had Builder as their dominant driver in their younger years, but now we sometimes find that Builder is their lowest motivator! This is not as odd as it might sound. Whilst Bill Gates, the richest man in the world (and who has never done a Map, incidentally!) once ran a company that was a commercial marvel, latterly his intention seems to be to give away a large proportion of that wealth to help eradicate malaria throughout the world. In short, what was once Builder has shifted up a gear to become Searcher.[18]

Thus, over the longer term certain what we call Growth motivators will become stronger (specific and circumstantial changes not withstanding). The three Growth motivators are, Searcher (meaning and purpose), Spirit (freedom and autonomy), and Creator (innovation and change). So, as you get older, and as you develop as a person, there is a high probability these motivators will become more important to you. This certainly seems the pattern in the case of Leon.

We see that Leon has two Growth motivators in his top three; and as these are likely to increase in strength, they are possibly a priority in terms of fulfilment. Leon, historically, was heavily motivated by money, competition and targets, and controlling the people within his business. This led to long hours of work. But now, as his marriage evolved with parenthood, these old patterns were now no longer fulfilling; note how dissatisfied he is with his number one motivator, Spirit, the desire for freedom.

Internal conflicts for Leon

Spirit v Director or in everyday language FREEDOM v CONTROL

The Map crystallised what Leon had been thinking for a while: his desire for personal freedom had overtaken his need for power, control, and influence. Therefore, he needed an exit plan. This was a big step.

Searcher v Builder or in everyday language MEANING v MONEY

Leon stated that currently this wasn't a conflict for him, as he was paid well for what he did and still found his work incredibly meaningful. This meant that whatever exit plan was devised needed to allow him to continue to earn and do what he found most meaningful. So in essence this is another example where a potential conflict turned out not to be present.

External conflicts

Leon explained that he was finding his potential exit route blocked through his relationship with his co-director with whom he had built the business. They were good friends and Leon felt both guilty about leaving his friend behind and also felt blocked to a degree with regards to having to agree the exit plan with Shaun.

The two external conflicts in play here were:

Director (Leon)	v	Friend (Shaun's map)
Spirit (Leon)	v	Defender (Shaun's map).

Shaun's need to keep things stable and secure and to keep things on an even keel financially were constraining Leon's plans for personal freedom and the changes required within the business to facilitate that.

ACTIVITY 8.9

Is there anyone you know at work whom you suspect to have opposing motivational preferences to you? If you are self-employed – a coach even – consider some client or supplier where this may be true. If so how could you use these ideas to become more skilled at influencing them?

The outcome

Through the coaching, Leon and Shaun agreed an exit plan whereby Leon would set up a new office in Singapore (their first overseas office) once he had assisted the London branch to a performance target.

This was successfully executed and now Leon is in the process of selling his share of the business to spend greater time with the family (meeting the growing Spirit motivator) and to do what he now finds more meaningful: himself pursuing a career in coaching (fuelling the growing and evolving Searcher motivator)!

As career coaches we want to boost the success of our clients; and this, from what we have already covered, is a complex issue. Rather than focusing, as most career coaches do, simply on promotion, getting ahead, and the usual symptoms of what constitutes a 'career', we, as Motivational Mapping coaches, are advocating a slightly different approach: what constitutes success itself is the first thing to determine – it's actually easy to be successful at what you subsequently discover has little value – and what that is must be defined partially by our motivational profile. In other words, by what we really want. That said, we have also advocated digging down at a deeper level, especially to one's core mission. Alongside all this we still have to be savvy and recognise that employers – if we wish to be employed – have requirements that either play to our strengths, or prove to be problematic for us; and as coaches we need to help our clients address these requirements.

Ultimately, this coaching for a career comes down to finding a fit between what we really want, or what has been called our "deep gladness",[19] and what the world hungers for us to offer it! Seven steps, then, may be useful for a career coach to review with their client:

1 What are your motivators – what do you want?
2 What is your mission, your verb, that you must stay focused on?
3 What subjects or topics[20] interest you?
4 In what sectors/fields do these subjects operate?
5 What role or occupation in this sector/field do you really like?
6 So what type of career would meet these criteria?
7 What organisations, if any, offer these kind of jobs and hire these kind of people? If none exists, then do you want to create such a position for yourself[21]?

ACTIVITY 8.10

Either review your own career through these seven steps or as a coach use them with one of your clients. Remember not to treat the questions as if they were some checklist to be gotten through, ticked off in a perfunctory fashion. All of these questions require sensitive thought and application, and most important of all: they require coherence. The difficulty for the coach is ensuring the answers in one area are consistent with those in another; here is where the core skill of listening is essential.

SEARCHER	Voluntary sector/charity; customer-facing role; mission-critical tasks/meaningful projects
SPIRIT	Lack of close supervision; ability to make own decisions/discretion; can prioritise own time
CREATOR	Problem-solving/developmental work; high change/challenge environments; stream of new initiatives
EXPERT	Technical positions; professional environments; high skill and/or knowledge jobs
BUILDER	Performance and reward clearly linked; commission, bonuses; above average rates of pay
DIRECTOR	Responsibility built into role; clear promotion and/or career prospects; control of resources
STAR	Clear job titles, visible recognition; hierarchical structure; perks linked to level within organisation
FRIEND	Strong team ethos; excellent social and "extra-curricular" activities; caring management
DEFENDER	Stable and secure organisation; predictable advancement within organisation; routine/repetitive work

Figure 8.6 Motivators and three qualities of work

We have looked in Figure 8.1 at the data which show how specific sectors attract certain motivational types. Now it would be good to reverse that pattern and show how certain motivators are perhaps best suited to certain types of occupation (see Figure 8.6).

ACTIVITY 8.11

Here is a useful activity to help you get more clarity on the kind of role – or the qualities within it – that would really suit you! Make a note of your top three motivators in column 1 of Figure 8.7. Then review the three qualities of work suggested in Figure 8.6 for each of your top three motivators. Write down in column 2 those that resonate as being relevant for you. For example, if Friend were in your top three and you reviewed its 'qualities', you might want 'Strong team ethos' and 'caring management' but be less concerned with 'Excellent social and extra-curricular activities'. So you'd write down the two you particularly want; or, maybe you just want the 'excellent social ...'; or, again you want all three or none. If Searcher is in the top three it is important for you to define what it is that you find meaningful, as from our experience this varies massively from person to person. Therefore, put down what resonates.

My top 3 motivators	Selected qualities from Figure 8.6	Type of situation suitable?

Figure 8.7 Motivators, qualities, and suitable situations

My top 3 motivators	Selected qualities from Figure 8.6	Type of situation suitable?
Defender	Stable, secure environment, predictable advancement	Corporation or Government Agency?
Star	Clear job titles	Management
Searcher	Customer facing role	Customer Services

Figure 8.8 Motivators, qualities and suitable situations: An example

When you have done that, consider column 3: What type of scenario or situation actually provides that sort of opportunity? Figure 8.8 gives an example of how this is done.

We see the conclusion from wanting a 'stable and secure organisation' means, inevitably, that we will want to pitch our efforts at larger corporates, or better still, large local or municipal authorities, or – better still – government employment where the risks of losing one's job are markedly reduced. If we start considering cach of our motivators in this way – viewing it from the perspective of the qualities that we want in our role or job – then a picture begins to emerge. In this case, with someone with Defender, Star, and Searcher – and often when Star is in the top three it occurs with Searcher – we see from the selection of qualities we need to consider a possible role within a corporation or government agency, which will certainly provide a clear and hierarchical management structure, and where there will be customer services that one can operate within. Given the motivators and qualities selected, conversely, the client would be ill-advised to start applying for a post in a start-up company or a small-to-medium sized business which invariably function in a 'seat-of-their-pants', 'all-hands-to-the-wheel' kind of way.

Finally, what are some good ideas to boost your career; ideas that really are proven to work? Here are six that can really help anyone develop faster.

1 Seek more training. Training is the key. Do we have the knowledge, the skills, the motivations to cope with the accelerating rate of change? Use the Pareto Principle: Seek to be in the top 20 per cent of the top 20 per cent – one of the top 4 per cent!

2   Review your motivation/commitment to your job every month. It's strange how nearly everyone has 100 per cent motivation when they first start a job. Suddenly, four years or four weeks or four days later, they don't. Don't wait till everyone else knows your heart's not in it.

3   Update your CV every 6 months. This increases your sense of control – which boosts your self-esteem, which – in turn – boosts your actual performance levels.

4   Start a diary. If that sounds too much hassle, then at least log daily what you've achieved. It's estimated that some 70 per cent of our self-talk is negative.[22] Concentrate on your achievements.

5   Actively request new tasks from your boss! Don't wait to be asked. Don't, in fact, be passive – like most people.

6   Imagine you are the boss. They have problems to solve – who can solve these problems for them – can you solve them now? The more problems you solve, the more they like, recommend, depend on and are likely to advance and reward you.

These ideas are suggestive for both client and coach; using them yourself or suggesting them to a client can make a big difference to future outcomes. It's certainly true, however, that we have not covered all there is to cover in career coaching or simply in the topic of careers itself; but we have provided here some key insights that Motivational Maps add to our understanding of the issue, and of the ability to generate effective change.

Summary

1   Different sectors tend to develop differing motivational profiles over time.
2   Verbs help us define our mission.
3   Employers consider about 10 different factors in employing anybody.
4   Usually two or three (Pareto) of these factors are critical.
5   Energy, or motivation, is almost certainly the single most important factor in a successful career.
6   Motivational Maps can be used to help gain greater clarity on career choices.
7   There is a seven-step process to bridge the gap between your 'deep gladness' and the world's hunger for it.
8   Each of the nine motivators has three defining qualities that help identify what we are looking for in our career options.
9   Six proven ideas can accelerate your career, if you use them.

Notes

1   Thanks are due to Shirley Thompson for her substantial help and advice in extracting these data: http://bit.ly/2tYlh0N.
2   Based on over 28,000 Maps we have found that whilst males and females share the Searcher motivator as their number 1 motivator, their second and third choices are different.

3 This should not be totally surprising for another important reason: the Searcher motivator is the one more concerned with and focused on the customer/client than any other. Given that organisations primarily exist - when they are functional - to serve the customer, it is hardly surprising that the Searcher should emerge as dominant in many cases.

4 *Start with Why*, Simon Sinek, Penguin (2009).

5 And we need to be clear here: we have given the sample size in each case because we recognise these findings are provisional and may change in the light of further data. It is important to keep in mind that the data anyway are not representational of the population, since it is often middle and senior managers who undertake Map programmes.

6 That this information predominantly reflects UK motivational trends is almost certain as the majority of Maps are done in the UK. But when in 2010 we looked at a small sample of European Maps - and we must stress, too small to be statistically significant - we found, for example, that in France the Friend motivator was in the top three. It would be wrong to say that Friend ultimately is a dominant motivator in France, but it seems that cultural and national factors may well cause large variance in profiles.

7 Again, in the sample of over 28,000 Maps, the Star as lowest motivator appeared in nearly 23 per cent of the profiles.

8 This is not the same as a lack of knowledge and skill set; but absence of motivation ultimately leads to burn-out - for one's heart isn't in the activity.

9 We will treat this as synonymous with purpose here, though some experts make a distinction.

10 In his book *What Colour is Your Parachute?*, Richard Bolles, Ten Speed Press (2001), lists 246 Skills as Verbs.

11 Or, as Dr Keith Selby once told me: Make it new, make it true, make it you!

12 According to Lou Adler, high levels of energy are the most important element in all success: *Power Hiring*, Nightingale Conant (2000). We are indebted to his ideas in *Power Hiring* for this section.

13 Whilst character is rarely the number 1 factor in a hire, its absence is a killer, for it means other great qualities are invalidated by character's absence. Warren Buffett expressed it this way: "We look for three things when we hire people. We look for intelligence, we look for initiative or energy, and we look for integrity. And if they don't have the latter, the first two will kill you, because if you're going to get someone without integrity, you want them lazy and dumb. I mean, you don't want a spark of energy out of them", http://read.bi/2vyNDTW.

14 Note that our simple grid of the 10 factors does not weight the scoring, which if it occurs will depend on the perception of the organisation of the relative importance of each of the factors. Candidates need to think carefully about what is important to a prospective employer and adjust their presentations accordingly.

15 See Chapter 5 for more on number ranges and their meaning.

16 The exception to this observation would be a 'false' result; we are not dealing with that possibility here except to say two things. First, they are rare in Motivational Mapping, since why would anyone want to conceal even from themselves their true motivators? But, second, they do occur, and within the system trained licensees can usually spot them as there are number sequences that indicate a contrived result.

17 For in-depth analysis of this correlation see Chapters 2 and 3 of *Mapping Motivation*, James Sale, Routledge (2016).

18 Always keep in mind, however, that no motivator is intrinsically superior to any other. In the case of Bill Gates, the assumed Builder motivator early on has certainly enabled the Searcher motivator later on. There is an interdependence, in other words.

19 Richard Bolles, ibid.

20 This may centre around skill clusters such as: manual-mechanical; analytical-research; creative-innovative; verbal-managerial; helping-guiding; or detail-numerical. Usually one has a strong predisposition in one area and maybe some ability in one or two others; but certainly not all six!

21 Clearly, motivational preferences speak volumes here. For example, from our experience with Motivational Maps, the Spirit motivator as a strong number 1 driver invariably indicates (keeping in mind the 2nd and 3rd preferences) a maverick, or independent, or entrepreneurial attitude to employment and having a 'job'.

22 'How Negative is Your "Mental Chatter"', Raj Raghunathan, *Psychology Today* (2013), http://bit.ly/2ukHRVT: "Even though people claim to hold themselves in high regard, the thoughts that spontaneously occur to them – their "mental chatter," so to speak – is mostly (up to 70 per cent) negative, a phenomenon that could be referred to as negativity dominance."

Conclusion

We have been on a long journey together in *Mapping Motivation for Coaching*, but not an exhaustive one. It is important to stress as we reach the end that this is not a book that reveals everything you need to know to become a coach; of course, along the way we have outlined the key concepts and ideas underpinning effective coaching, but always we have tried where possible to make the Motivational Map our focal point for the practice of coaching. This is because we believe that Motivational Maps open up a whole new vista for the development of coaching. Further, we notice ourselves as we progress through these chapters that a certain and important theme emerges: namely, that knowing a few things well, at a deep level, is far superior than knowing all that can be known but at a superficial pitch.

To take some examples. Knowing motivation and Maps really well is vital because motivation – energy – fuels all that we do. Thus, the precision that the Maps afford on this topic can only be a massive benefit in galvanising the client, and enabling them to gain that extra performance boost that so often constitutes what has been called the 'winning edge'.[1] High levels of energy are the universal success factor in all situations, and to know this and to make it core in one's coaching practice and in one's own life is to experience benefits out of all proportion to the simple idea behind it.

But alongside that central concern of ours we have illustrated the real significance of the Pareto Principle, and how using it in all situations increases both our focus – by concentrating on the one or two things that really make a difference – and our efficiency – by spending less time on the 'trivial many'. Following the pioneering work of Richard Koch and others on this topic, we hope our demonstration of its relevance to Maps and performance – and so to productivity – will be duly noted and acted on by all coaches.

Then, too, we have NLP (Neuro Linguistic Programming) and its relevance to coaching and to Maps. We have tried in all the various chapters to give a flavour of NLP practice, even when not specifically using one of their ideas or techniques. This is especially so when dealing with the blocks of time and money, and even more so when dealing with people as the barrier to our success, whether that be because of self-limiting beliefs holding us back in our dealings with others, or self-sabotaging us, or whether we are actually confronting directly the obstacles and difficulties people sometimes put in our way. Mapping Motivation and NLP have some acute angles on how to deal with these situations.

Finally, we have tried to cover aspects of changing our values and, as values are specialised beliefs that we attach emotional significance to, there could hardly be a more transformative topic. Again, Maps have so much to offer in our understanding of this mission critical area of our lives, though ironically we save mission, establishing our mission, till last when we review how coaching and Mapping Motivation can help us with our careers.

If we had written another chapter it might have been called 'Coaching for consciousness', for that perhaps is also an underlying theme of the book. Quite apart from the obvious benefits of coaching in enabling the client to perform at a higher level, to become more successful, there is that developmental aspect of coaching which returns us to the realisation that increasing self-awareness,[2] or consciousness, is at the heart of everything. We cannot improve, be better people, until we become aware of our current condition and see in the mind's eye – imagine even – a future in which we have become someone else. This is at the core of living.

And it is exemplified in the life of Dr David Servan-Schreiber who died in 2011. He was a neuro-scientist who struggled with brain cancer for about 20 years before finally succumbing. In his best-selling book, *Anti-Cancer*, he writes:

> To describe the very foundation of the life force, Aristotle speaks about 'entelechy' (the need for self-fulfilment that starts with the seed and comes to full fruition in the tree). Jung describes a 'process of individuation', transforming the person into a different human being from all others, capable of fully expressing his or her unique potential. Abraham Maslow, the founder of the human potential movement, refers to 'self-actualisation'. The spiritual traditions encourage 'awakening' by developing the unique – in other words, the sacred – in the self.[3]

It is to his high calling that *Mapping Motivation for Coaching* is seeking to contribute.

Notes

1   The winning edge is a concept often referred to by sports coaches in which they note that the winning competitor often wins by only a fraction of a second, and so are only marginally superior to whoever comes in second, but the rewards for being 'first' can be double, treble or quadruple, or even more, the prize for being second. This imbalance - an example actually of Pareto again - occurs in all competitive fields: sales being a classic example. In recruitment, of course, the effect is even more pronounced, as often a great candidate who comes 'second' gets no prize at all.
2   "Awareness, as the Buddha ... insisted, truly has universal effects" - Dr David Servan-Schreiber, *Anti-Cancer*, Penguin (2011).
3   Dr David Servan-Schreiber, ibid.

Resources

This section of the book is designed to help you find more information about motivation, coaching and Motivational Maps. It is not comprehensive and will be updated in subsequent editions.

Information about Motivation Maps Ltd and Motivational Maps

Motivational Maps Ltd was founded in 2006. Its Motivational Map is ISO accredited: ISO 17065: http://www.irqao.org/PDF/C11364-31620.pdf.

The company website can be found at www.motivationalmaps.com and enquiries should be addressed to info@motivationalmaps.com

James Sale, the author, can be found at www.jamessale.co.uk

and his LinkedIn profile is: https://uk.linkedin.com/in/jamesmotivationsale

Bevis Moynan, the co-author, can be found at Magenta Coaching Solutions: www.magentacs.co.uk in Cambridgeshire, UK.

His LinkedIn profile is: https://www.linkedin.com/in/bevis-moynan-b468681b

For more information on how to become an Accredited Mapping Motivation Coach contact Bevis at info@magentacs.co.uk

There are currently four different Motivational Maps available, although this book covers just one of them, the Motivational Map.

1 The Motivational Map is for individuals and employees to discover what motivates them and how motivated they are; this produces a 15-page report on the individual.
2 The Motivational Team Map, which the forthcoming book, *Mapping Motivation for Management* (Routledge, 2019) is largely devoted to. This is a 22+ page report which synthesises the individual maps from any number of people, and reveals what the overall motivational scores are. It is ideal for team leaders and managers.
3 The Motivational Organisational Map produces a 44-page report and synthesises the information from any number of team maps be they from the whole organisation or a section of the whole organisation. Ideal for senior managers to understand how to implement their strategies through people. In 2020

Routledge will release *Mapping Motivation for Strategy and Change*, which will cover aspects of this diagnostic.

4   The Motivational Youth Map is different from the other Maps in that it has three outputs: one for the student, one for the teacher and one for the parent; all designed to help motivate the student to succeed at school and college. Ideal for 11–18 year olds and schools and colleges looking to motivate their students. There is also the Youth Group Map.

The Motivational Map questionnaire is in seven different languages: English, German, French, Italian, Greek, Lithuanian, and Portuguese.

Motivational Maps Ltd has licensed over 400 consultants, coaches and trainers to deliver the Map products in 14 countries. There are 5 Senior Practitioners of Maps in the UK:

UK Senior Practitioners

Bevis Moynan, co-author of this book, www.magentacs.co.uk, Cambridgeshire

Susannah Brade-Waring, Aspirin Business Solutions, www.aspirinbusiness.com, Dorset

Kate Turner, Motivational Leadership, www.motivationalleadership.co.uk, Wiltshire

Jane Thomas, Premier Life Skills, www.premierlifeskills.co.uk, Dorset

Mark Turner and David Livsey, www.motivationalmapseducation.com, Midlands/Yorkshire

There is 1 International Senior Practitioners of Maps

Akeela Davis, Courageous Business Culture, www.courageousbusinessculture.com, Canada

More information on James Sale can be found on his personal website: www.jamessale.co.uk

Motivational Maps Resources can be found on www.motivationalmaps.com/Resources

Other Key Books on Motivation, Coaching and Personal Development

Nine books we like on coaching, NLP, and related topics are:

The Little Book of Big Coaching Models, Bob Bates, Pearson (2015)
The 80/20 Principle, Richard Koch, Nicholas Brealey (1997)
NLP in 21 Days, Harry Alder and Beryl Heather, Piatkus (1998)
Authentic Happiness, Martin Seligman, Random House (2002)

The Road to Character, David Brooks, Random House (2015)
Happier, Tal Ben-Shahar, The Observer (2008)
The Happiness Advantage, Shawn Achor, Random House (2010)
What Colour is Your Parachute?, Richard Bolles, Ten Speed Press (2016)
Coaching and Mentoring, Nigel MacLennan, Gower (1999)

Index